Building
Conservation
Philosophy

Building Conservation Philosophy

John Earl

THIRD EDITION

DONHEAD

First published in 1996 by the College of Estate Management, Reading
Second edition 1997
Reprinted 2001

This third edition published in the United Kingdom in 2003 by Donhead Publishing in association with the College of Estate Management, Reading.

Donhead Publishing
Lower Coombe
Donhead St Mary
Shaftesbury
Dorset SP7 9LY
Tel: +44 (0)1747 828422
www.donhead.com

ISBN 1 873394 56 X

Designed by Linda Reed and Associates, Shaftesbury, Dorset
Printed in Great Britain by J.H. Haynes & Co. Ltd. Sparkford, Somerset

A CIP catalogue record is available for this book from the British Library

Library of Congress Cataloguing in Publication Data
A catalog record for this book has been requested

Cover illustrations: The restored Royal Opera House with the reconstructed Floral Hall alongside (1858 and 1860 by Edward M Barry); they were incorporated in 1999 into a new opera house complex extending over an entire city block (see page 118).

Contents

PART III MEANS AND MANNER OF PRESERVATION

Foreword

No better *vade-mecum* than the present text could be put in the hands of those concerned with building conservation in the English-speaking world, be they budding students or seasoned professionals. In a brief compass, John Earl has brought together all the critical facts, all the quandaries and all the essential documents which anyone tackling this intricate subject needs to ponder. Here is a book which seems to be on its way to becoming a quiet classic. And that for a simple reason: it makes the reader think.

An academic might have christened such a work a theory of building conservation. Relying instead on the practical wisdom he learnt finding a fair future for old buildings on behalf of the Greater London Council's Historic Buildings Division and of the Theatres Trust, the author has chosen to speak of a philosophy. In one of his opening quotations, that term is glossed as about 'calmness of temper' as well as about principles. His reasonable, even and undogmatic tone makes the text immediately attractive and accessible. Step by step, we are taken through the maze of building conservation, and asked why we wish to conserve (motive), what it is we are trying to protect (mostly, but by no means always, 'monuments'), and how it is all to be gone about (means).

The means naturally take the lion's share of the argument. Policies, polemics, passing fashions and solid advances in thinking and technique are all laid out in the light of accumulating experience; and a broadly conservative approach to the historic fabric of the nation is vindicated. But at every point John Earl is at pains to remind us that the conservation of architecture is not primarily a discipline based on rules or techniques. It relies for its appeal upon strength of feeling about history, beauty and memory, and its practical aim is the reconciliation of different interests. Each case must be scrutinised on its merits, and to each the reader is bidden to bring 'thoughtful rather than reflexive judgements'.

Building conservation is often caricatured by its opponents as a rigid and ossifying business. Yet one thing that emerges from these pages is the fast-developing nature of its philosophy and techniques. That is one reason why the inclusion in the appendices of a raft of conservation manifestos, charters and precepts, many now hard to track down, is of such value. Reading these, one is struck by the shift not just from the SPAB *Manifesto* of 1877 to the *Venice Charter* of 1964, but also from the *Venice Charter* to the *Burra Charter*. (This last, an Australian document, reminds us how often recent advances in thinking on conservation have come from countries where the built heritage is, by European standards, mostly quite young.) Nor are the changes since the original 1996 edition of this book less marked. In the past few years, understanding of the ecological value of looking after older buildings has developed by leaps and bounds, so that building conservation has at last taken its place within the wider arguments about sustainability, as is now reflected in Chapter 5. In some ways we seem also more interested now in the total historic context and value of places, and less obsessed with isolated works of architecture, a point taken up in Chapter 10. On the other hand, with the cult of individualism and of the celebrity rampant in our society, the obsession with 'design' and the 'masterpiece' is stronger now than ever. Here is one of the many continuing paradoxes of conservation – a supremely human, various and sometimes even contradictory endeavour.

In some circles in Britain, there is a feeling abroad now that the important battles in architectural conservation have been won, and all that is needed is to maintain a cautious line and an efficient system for looking after what has now been identified and is well enough safeguarded. The reader has only to turn to the last words of John Earl's 'Last Words' to appreciate that an articulate defence of the built heritage has still to be actively and constantly mounted. That defence must always base its appeal on reasons of the heart. This book shows the necessity for that again and again.

Andrew Saint
University of Cambridge
December 2002

Author's Preface

This book started life in 1990 as a teaching text for students taking the RICS post-graduate diploma in building conservation. It was published as a book by the College of Estate Management in 1996 and is now presented in further revised and enlarged form. The text has been reconsidered and reordered throughout in the light of the helpful comments received from educators, students and reviewers and substantial additions have been made to give attention to matters either not covered or less effectively covered in earlier editions. Chapters 9,10 and 11, in particular, contain much new material on for example, contextual issues and questions of economic sustainability. The Appendices have been updated and added to and my commentary on the historic (and truly remarkable) 1946 *Instructions* to listing investigators has been greatly extended. Many readers have remarked to me on the usefulness of the illustrations in clarifying arguments in the text and have wished for more. Their number has now, therefore, been substantially increased.

The modern literature of building conservation is expanding at a daunting rate – or so it seems to anyone old enough to remember when there were no more than one or two books to turn to. You were lucky in the 1950s if you had a dog-eared copy of Powys on *The Repair of Ancient Buildings* and the opportunity to gather variably trustworthy bits of technical know-how and traditional lore by oral transmission. Today we are drenched with published information.

When I first set out to write on this subject, I confidently expected to find a mass of recent texts that I could raid for ideas. To my surprise, I was led rapidly back to nineteenth and early twentieth-century works. Jokilehto's *History of Architectural Conservation* has since made up for decades of past neglect, but that outstanding work of scholarship did not become generally available until 1999 and there is still very little designed specifically to serve the needs of students approaching the subject for the first time.

This is not, of course, to say that there has been no recent discussion of conservation philosophy. Practitioners, speaking or writing of the problems they have faced in particular cases, invariably explain the philosophy, which has guided them. Academic works on the psychological roots of conservation movements, scientific studies of the pathology of buildings and techniques of conservation repair – nearly all have some philosophical content. Few of them, however, discuss the philosophical issues themselves at length. Most of them adopt an approach that assumes a broad consensus on the most fundamental philosophical questions.

It seemed to me that students setting off on a career in conservation needed to start from a position of inquiry, rather than acceptance. They are hardly likely to embark on so demanding a course if they have not already decided to their own satisfaction that the work is thoroughly worthwhile. They are not, however, in my opinion, likely to become good conservators if they do not, from the outset, ask themselves: 'Why do we do this at all? What convincing case can be presented for singling out some buildings and treating them in special ways? What, in precise terms, is such special treatment designed to achieve? Are we working toward the same kind of end result in every case? On what authority do we justify interference with the freedom of owners to do as they please with their own property? And on what grounds do we argue that one treatment is acceptable in conservation terms while another is unacceptable?' – and so on.

Such questions had been thoroughly aired – in fact, furiously argued – before 1900. Very few really new issues are being discussed in the first decade of the twenty first century which were not being agonised over in the nineteenth century by the Scrape and Anti-Scrape factions, by Viollet-le-Duc, Ruskin, Scott, Morris and Lubbock and their contemporaries. What has happened since 1905, when Baldwin Brown wrote the common-sensical summing-up contained in the first 56 pages of his *Care of Ancient Monuments*, is that public demand for the better preservation of the past has grown hugely and a consensus has developed among experts of the general desirability of minimum intervention (it is not really as simple as that, but the generalisation is not too misleading). At the same time, daily experience has shown that the ways in which practice matches up to what the most skilled practitioners preach are coloured by a host of considerations which no rigid philosophy can provide for.

It is not possible – and if it were possible it would not be helpful – to offer sets of commandments to be committed to memory. I have tried to give students a very basic understanding of the history of movements to preserve old buildings, the ambitions which have driven such movements at different times and the philosophical arguments which have surrounded them for the last two hundred years.

I hope that this may lead them to question their own opinions and actions and bring them to a clearer understanding of what – as practitioners – they will be doing. This book has no other purpose.

John Earl

Three influential figures in the history of preservation movements in Britain

i (above left) John Ruskin (1819–1900). Architectural theorist and the most influential early campaigner against the destructive 'restoration' of old buildings.

ii (above right) William Morris (1834–1896). Founder of the Society for the Protection of Ancient Buildings 1877 and author of its *Manifesto*.

iii (left) Sir John Lubbock (Lord Avebury) initiated the first Ancient Monuments Bill and guided the London County Council in its first moves to record and preserve old buildings.

Conservation

Whatever is good in its kinde ought to be preserv'd in respect for antiquity, as well as our present advantage, for destruction can be profitable to none but such as live by it.
Nicholas Hawksmoor: letter to Dr George Clarke, Fellow of All Souls, Oxford (on the rebuilding of the College), 17 February 1715

Philosophy

Philo'sophy ... The principles underlying any department of knowledge ... reasoning ... calmness of temper ...
Chambers' Dictionary

Acknowledgements

Nearly everyone I have ever worked with has contributed in some way to the making of this book. I am particularly grateful to my ex-colleagues in the LCC and GLC Historic Buildings Division for discussion and argument over a period of thirty years. They provided me with the best education anyone could have wished for.

This new edition has benefited further from discussions with Henry Russell, Director of the RICS post-graduate diploma in building conservation at the College of Estate Management and his predecessor in that role, John Gleeson. Jill Pearce and Dorothy Newberry of Donhead Publishing have been extremely helpful, tolerating my many second and third thoughts with great patience. I am also indebted to reviewers of the 1996 edition for a number of thoughtful observations that have led me to revise or extend my text. Clare Finn kindly read my comments on fresco conservation in Chapter 5 and Philip Venning read the manuscript of the 1996 edition. I adopted a number of their suggestions, but any errors, omissions or flawed arguments are mine alone.

The text of the *Canadian Code* is reproduced by kind permission of the Canadian Association for Conservation of Cultural Property and that of the *Burra Charter* by kind permission of ICOMOS Australia.

Most of the pictures come from my own collection. I am grateful for permission to use the following: 7.2a and b (English Heritage, National Monuments Record); cartoon at 9.1 (*Punch*); 9.6a and b, 9.7 a and b (Corporation of London, London Metropolitan Archives). Care has been taken to find copyright holders wherever possible. Apologies are due to any I may have inadvertently missed.

PART I

Introduction

In our own country the task of the apologist is particularly difficult,
for it is generally looked upon as sentimentality or weakness to put the
interests of preservation higher than some utilitarian consideration of
the moment and it is held in some quarters as an article of faith that
any practical demand may claim priority over the ideal plea of the
lover of monuments or of nature.
G Baldwin Brown, *The Care of Ancient Monuments*, 1905

These old buildings do not belong to us only; … they have belonged to
our forefathers and they will belong to our descendants unless we play
them false. They are not … our property, to do as we like with. We are
only trustees for those that come after us.
William Morris, 1889

(On the proposed demolition of Northumberland House which stood in
the path of a new road):

Would not our modern Haussmans do well to recall sometimes to
mind the old nursery rhyme –
     'What you cannot make
     You should not break.'
Anon, *Graphic* (periodical) editorial, 1873

A man has no scale unless he stands against bricks and stones erected
before he was born.
Beryl Bainbridge (quoting her father), *Observer* 9, March 1997

Les longs souvenirs font les grands peuples. (Long memories make
great peoples)
Montalambert, c 1830

CHAPTER 1

Guiding Lights

This book (it is really a series of essays) is about ideas rather than techniques. Its aim is not to indoctrinate the reader with a particular set of articles of absolute faith. It begins by discussing why buildings are preserved and looks at the philosophical problems surrounding any act of preservation. It then attempts to guide the reader toward an analytical and self-critical approach in the search for defensible solutions to these problems.

The conservation of historic structures is not a mechanical activity controlled by hard and fast formulae which, correctly applied, will produce demonstrably correct solutions. The decisions having to be made daily by the practitioner raise philosophical questions at every turn.

What, in fact, are we setting out to do when we embark on the care of a monument, historic building or complete historic environment? What (for a start) do we mean by monument or historic building? Why should such buildings be treated differently from other buildings – and how differently? What precisely are our motives in preserving or conserving rather than merely maintaining and how should those motives influence actions? Is every part of an old fabric so sacred that it must at all costs be propped and secured, whatever its state? Is it permissible to replace outworn or disfigured elements and, if so, should the replacements be exact copies of the original work or should they be clearly discernible from it? And in this context, what does original mean? How should the practical consequences of an unavoidable change of use (or an environmental change) be accommodated? And in considering questions of this kind, should we expect the answers to vary with the age, nature and external circumstances of the building?

Practitioners who attempt to undertake conservation work without having given serious thought to such issues will find themselves in a rudderless ship. It is not simply a matter of doing as much work as the money permits, with more money leading to better results. Indeed, the reverse may be true. It is sometimes better in conservation terms to do nothing or nearly nothing. An understanding of the philosophy of conservation (and, for reasons which will become clear, we should, perhaps, rather say philosophies of conservation) provides a necessary frame of reference against which judgements – often quite finely balanced – can be made.

The conservation of historic structures is an extremely demanding discipline. Philosophy provides guiding lights. The practitioner must provide the solutions – and be prepared to defend them against critical examination.

> *I have found that it is not wise to lay down dogmatic rules, for when they are made one is apt to be confronted by a case where they do not work.*
> A R Powys, *Repair of Ancient Buildings*, 1929, reprinted 1981

Powys's advice related to techniques of repair, but it is sound advice in relation to most aspects of work with historic buildings.

CHAPTER *2*

Approach to the Subject

We should begin by examining the historical development of conservation philosophies up to the present time, with references drawn from contemporary writings. Some of the more important modern policy statements will be quoted at length in the Appendices.

The discussion of specific issues, which accounts for the rest of the book, is conducted so far as possible in plain English. The few specialised terms needed are explained as they arise. All other words are used here with their common dictionary meanings, or meanings which will be clear in context. It would probably be helpful at the outset however, to clear away some of the litter which has accumulated around the words preservation and conservation.

Most dictionaries relate the second to the first. To 'preserve' is 'to keep safe from harm ... to maintain, keep up ... guard against decay'. To 'conserve' is 'to preserve, retain, keep entire'.

Until a relatively short time ago, in common professional usage historic buildings tended to be *preserved* and museum objects and art works *conserved*. In some contexts the two terms have now changed places. The surge of public concern which led to the reform of the protective laws in the mid-1960s prompted a great deal of propagandist writing in which a new distinction was drawn (especially by architectural writers) between the museum preservation of buildings in supposedly 'frozen-in-time' states and the enlightened conservation of imaginatively adapted buildings 'in the environment'. The former was represented as a sterile, negative process and the latter as a creative, forward-looking activity.

However useful this artificial black-and-white contrast may have been in early environmental campaigns (and I do not regard the case as proven), it is not helpful in the present context. In this book, except when quoting historical sources, preservation has its simple dictionary meaning, with no pejorative overtones. Conservation is used when a rather more inclusive term is needed, embracing not only physical preservation but also all those other activities, which the practitioner must engage in to be successful in 'preserving, retaining and keeping entire'.

Two charters quoted in the Appendices (*Burra* and the *Canadian Code*) have, for their own purposes, proposed more precise definitions for these and other terms, but you can look at them later.

Now read on. In the following chapters the philosophical background to conservation is considered under three main headings:

- Motive – Why do we wish to conserve?
- Monument – What are we trying to conserve?
- Manner and Means – How should it be done?

The alliterative keywords are adopted simply to aid memory. They are not watertight subject headings. The first two have to be considered together as two sides of the same question. The third has been answered in different ways in different times and places. The final section of this book re-examines all these issues in the light of modern attitudes and policy statements.

PART II

The Nature of Monuments: Motives for Preservation

CHAPTER *3*

Utility

Maintenance instead of reconstruction; that is the general aim of conservation.
Hermann Muthesius, 1902

Use it or lose it.
Modern health warning

The commonest reason for preserving old buildings (leave aside for the moment the question of historic interest) is that they are useful resources, capable of serving a modern purpose. This may seem absurdly obvious, but it is often forgotten.

Buildings have always been erected with some degree of permanence in mind. Whilst in most past ages the imposition of any sort of stay on the demolition of ordinary workaday buildings would have been looked upon with blank incomprehension, one need look no farther than the nearest town, village or farmstead to see evidence of the fact that, while beneficial use can be sustained, a building will be cared for. Even the most unexceptional building will continue to be repaired for as long as the owner thinks that it is useful or can be made so at reasonable cost.

In some cases it is now necessary to add 'and so long as the owner does not see the chance of a windfall profit which might accrue from demolition'; but there is an abundance of evidence that long life, if not permanence, has generally been regarded as a desirable attribute. With proper maintenance the life of most kinds of buildings can be extended almost indefinitely. In fact, at its simplest, preservation is synonymous with prudent maintenance – the slow and continuous replacement of that which has decayed and the protection of that which would otherwise decay.

A building usually reaches the end of its (so-called) 'natural life' as a result of external economic forces and operational obsolescence rather than because it has ceased to be capable of repair. An example of this process at work could be seen in the 1970s in the rapid decay and demolition of many hundreds of sturdily engineered and once well-maintained warehouse buildings in abandoned dock areas. They had not become unmaintainable. They were simply redundant. When, in such circumstances, particular buildings are singled out for continued care in new uses, it is safe to assume that some motive other than the owner's self-interest has been at work.

The ways in which the rights of private ownership have been restrained by preservation laws will be dealt with later. At this point we are concerned with underlying motives rather than legislative apparatus. In making a closer examination of these motives and their consequences (in terms of practice) we must begin to look at the kinds of buildings on which preservation efforts have tended to focus.

CHAPTER 4

The Creation and Preservation of Monuments

Celebratory and magnificent

I would have the Temple made so beautiful that the imagination should not be able to form an idea of any place more so, and I would have every part so contrived and adorned as to fill the beholders with awe and amazement...
Leone Battista Alberti, *De Re Aedificatoria (Ten Books of Architecture)* Book VII C, III (1485). Trans. James Leoni, 1726

The first and clearest case (for protection) is that of the building which is a work of art, the product of a distinct and outstanding creative mind.
Ministry of Town and Country Planning, *Instructions to Listing Investigators*, 1946

We have observed that most owners try to prolong building life for uncomplicated practical reasons, but it is also obviously true that some buildings, from the moment they were conceived, were marked out for preservation in a rather more special sense. Temples, cathedrals, palaces, memorials, centres of learning, centres of government, great auditoria, buildings associated with the rituals of religion and power or expressive of pride in national or cultural achievement have always been surrounded by material symbols and architectural display. A distinguished twentieth-century conservation authority classified these as 'intended monuments'. The fact that in comparatively recent times there has been a disinclination to create such deliberately monumental buildings is as yet insignificant in historical terms.

Buildings like the Parthenon, the Pantheon, Trajan's Column, Salisbury Cathedral, the Taj Mahal, the British Museum, the Paris (Garnier) Opera, Lenin's Tomb, Ceausescu's Palace or the Statue of Liberty were not erected with a limited life in view. Some of them may have a continuing practical service to perform, but utility is certainly not the sole reason for their existence. They are celebratory monuments, invested with symbolic significance and manifestly intended to be more or less permanent. The greatest of them have – and often had from the time of their completion – special custodians or surveyors to the fabric. The least have some claim to be considered as works of art, or works of deliberate 'historical landmarking', in their own right.

4.1a and 4.1b The Pantheon, Rome (AD118–129) (right) and the Paris Opera (Charles Garnier 1862–75) (below) were created to serve specific purposes, but they were also conceived as celebratory monuments. For such buildings, preservation becomes an issue from the moment of their completion.

1. – PARIS. – L'Opéra

Construit par Charles GARNIER (1861-1874). Académie Nationale de Musique. Superficie : 11.235 mq.
La scène mesure 15 m. de hauteur et autant de largeur. La salle contient 2.300 places.
L'emplacement a coûté 10 millions, la construction 37 millions.

The care of first-rank celebratory monuments is to some degree a matter of pride for the society or the stratum of society that produced them and, while that society remains stable, their fabrics are likely to be repaired and serviced to an exemplary standard. Some such buildings go through a period when they are undervalued, politically unacceptable or architecturally unfashionable, but if they survive these risks they tend to return permanently to national monument status. St Pancras Station, the Albert Memorial and the Eiffel Tower are obvious examples.

4.2 Some buildings have celebration as their main *raison d'être* but, from the beginning, excite controversy, rather than an immediate and general desire for their protection. Public opinion, political and social change, may profoundly affect their prospects for preservation. The Eiffel Tower (Gustave Eiffel) built for the Paris Universal Exhibition of 1889 and, at the time, the tallest building in the world, was detested by many French intellectuals. It is now regarded as a symbol of the city and an international monument of engineering (see also 11.2a for another building that weathered a similar period of unpopularity).

Clear evidence of the desire both to create and preserve celebratory monuments can be found in all historical periods:

> *In the classical world, no sooner had the fresh impulse of the formative arts of Greece died down, than we find the older Hellenic monuments preserved in honour … Of nearer kinship to the modern care of monuments is the conservation of the relics of Roman Antiquity by the more enlightened Teutonic chieftains. Cassiodorus served in this department Theodoric of Rome … (Theodoric the Ostrogoth, d 526 AD)*
> G Baldwin Brown, *The Care of Ancient Monuments*, 1905

4.3 Henry VII Chapel, Westminster Abbey, was certainly intended from its birth to be a permanent monument. The Renaissance initiated a period of general indifference to even the finest examples of gothic art, but by the second half of the eighteenth century, the chapel was seen as an object of wonder, to be jealously preserved.

The whole of Henry the Seventh's chapel, both external and internal, is so extremely fine and so exquisite a model of Gothick architecture that it is sincerely to be wished that no modern hand might ever be suffered to touch it, but as the teeth of time have already destroyed many parts of its exterior ornaments it ought to be repaired before it is too late, but with a most scrupulous adherence to its original form; not an ornament or single member should suffer the least alteration and if it was possible to build a case for the whole to prevent all further injuries, it would be doing no more than this amazing piece of art richly merits.

The more modern Goths have disfigured it in the most shameful manner, with such things as might well enough become a Lord Mayor's shew, but are in this place both mean and contemptible.
John Gwynn, *London and Westminster Improved*, 1766

Rare and curious

Buildings which do not immediately declare themselves to be deliberately created celebratory monuments can move into this class and excite interest and a desire to preserve as if they were monuments in a more formal sense. Most obviously, the simple fact of survival – especially survival from a distant, legendary past, with or without benefit of scholarly authentication – may make a building an object of rarity or curiosity. Stonehenge was regarded with awe long before its significance began to be understood.

4.4a When the grounds of Studley Royal were landscaped in 1720–40, picturesque ornaments like this 'Temple of Piety' were created to appeal to a not too precisely defined romantic past. In 1768 the adjoining estate was purchased and the ruins of Fountains Abbey were preserved as the architectural climax of the entire landscaping scheme.

4.4b The eighteenth-century treatment of Fountains Abbey illustrates one of the many ways in which the desire to preserve has found expression. Objects of great antiquity, prehistoric and Roman remains and the ruins of mediaeval buildings, were amongst the first to excite protective interest, as much for the sentiments they evoked as for their authenticity. They were also the first to be accorded scholarly study and the first in Britain to secure statutory protection. Nevertheless the schedule attached to the first Ancient Monuments Act of 1882 did not include even Fountains Abbey, despite the fact that it had become the finest of all picturesque ruins. Today the preservation of such ruins can raise finely balanced philosophical questions in meeting the competing demands of systematic investigation, scientific conservation, aesthetic presentation and (not least) explanation. In this case, what has to be preserved and presented today are the substantial architectural remains of a great Cistercian Abbey, the visible evidence of the trauma of the Dissolution and the delights of eighteenth-century landscape artistry.

In Athens on the Areopagus there is to this day a relic of antiquity with a mud roof. The hut of Romulus on the Capitol is a significant reminder of the fashions of old times.
Vitruvius, De Architectura *(Ten Books of Architecture)*, Book II C.I (1st century BC). Trans. Morris Hicky Morgan, 1914

Rich as our land is in historical monuments there is none more remarkable than the White Horse…
Thomas Hughes in *The Scouring of the White Horse*, 1857

The horse at first view is enough to raise the admiration of every curious spectator.
Rev. Francis Wise, 1738

4.5 The Uffington White Horse is another monument whose interest is many-layered. Whatever scholarly investigation may establish (or propose) about its origin and meaning, its emotional impact on many generations of ordinary observers, as a mysterious and profoundly evocative work of ancient art, has been crucial to its survival. The engraving shows one of its occasional scourings, undertaken as a local social event.

When Thomas Hughes was writing of the pastime of scouring the White Horse of Uffington (which, if one knew more of its origin, could well have been included above as a celebratory monument) it was revered either as the steed of St George, killer of the dragon, or as a memorial of the Battle of Ashdown, AD 871. The fact that it has been proved almost certainly to be of the late Bronze Age is, in a way, neither here nor there. It has always been a fascinating and mysterious object to all who saw it. More recently, the first visible fragments of the Rose Playhouse discovered on Bankside in 1989 excited a preservation campaign during which, deep emotional responses to its associations were quite as important as the scholarly interpretation of the remains.

4.6 Highgate Cemetery. Attitudes to the past are still greatly coloured by sentiment and this is not, by any means, to be regretted. The conservator can, however, be faced with critical decisions over what is generally thought to be aesthetically pleasing and what is necessary for preservation. An overgrown tomb can be a deeply satisfying sight but, left to itself, this one will be completely covered within a year. Intervention is unavoidable if the monument is to be seen, let alone effectively preserved.

Commemorative and associative

Historical associations can also promote a comparatively modest or utilitarian building to the status of a revered monument. A building which embodies a significant achievement – the iron bridge at Coalbrookdale – or a house associated with a great figure – Shakespeare, Rembrandt, Mozart or (nearer to our own time) Churchill – will, however humble its appearance, evoke strong passions and become a symbol of national or cultural identity, celebrated and cherished.

Wolfgang Amadeus MOZART (1756–1791) composed his first
symphony here in 1764
Blue Plaque on the front of No 180 Ebury Street, Westminster

*First amongst these (Midland districts) in the evolution of the British
Industrial Revolution was the westernmost … with its focal point at
Coalbrookdale and appropriately symbolised by the Iron Bridge of
1777, the so-called 'Stonehenge of the Industrial Revolution'.*
R A Buchanan, *Industrial Archaeology in Britain*, 1972

*Benjamin Britten's music studio, with its view across his beloved
Suffolk countryside is no architectural gem, but its importance as a
piece of our cultural heritage cannot be denied.*
Tessa Jowell, Culture Secretary, on listing Britten's plain brick garden shed,
October 2002

4.7a Modest buildings have excited a desire
to preserve, especially if they were associated
with famous people or historical events.
Dickens's house in Doughty Street is a single
dwelling in an unelaborate late Georgian
terrace. The terrace is now protected in its
own right, but the associations of this one
house have attracted literary pilgrims from all
parts of the world since at least the 1920s.

4.7b Even fictional associations may be sufficiently powerful to excite the urge for
protection. This old house in north Kent first attracted attention, long before the
initiation of the statutory lists, as the supposed original of Gargery's Forge in
Dickens's *Great Expectations*. The picture shows it in 1971, looking convincingly
ramshackle. It is now safely listed and so splendidly manicured that it is difficult to
believe that Joe Gargery can ever have passed its door.

4.8 A building may become a memorial of past conditions as well as past styles of architecture. The emotions aroused by this Soup Kitchen for the Jewish Poor in Spitalfields, are sure to vary with the generation and the degree of personal involvement felt by the observer. The really elderly may have painful family memories that they would prefer to bury. Their descendants, revisiting the neighbourhood where their great-grandparents grew up, may feel a glow of pride in a physical record of social adversity overcome by self-help. Young Jews are more likely to view such a building with simple curiosity about a past they may feel they should know more about. Whatever one's viewpoint, this is a building that speaks from the past in an uniquely powerful way.

The reader will see at once that a monument may commend itself for preservation for more reasons than one. The iron bridge is not just of symbolic or associative interest. Its status as a rarity is obvious and it also has some claims to be included in the next group.

Exemplary and instructive

An important class of building that has attracted protective activity may be labelled exemplary. All old buildings can be studied for what they reveal about the past but historically, architectural exemplars were amongst the first to be singled out in this way.

The Renaissance was accompanied by a great surge of interest in even the most fragmentary remains of Antiquity which could be measured and analysed in order to advance the cause of modern architecture by returning to the perfect forms and proportions (as they were conceived to be) of the past.

> *... I proposed to myself Vitruvius for my master and guide ... and set myself to search into the reliques of all the ancient edifices that, in spite of time and the cruelty of the barbarians, yet remain; and finding them much more worthy of observation than at first I had imagined, I began very minutely with the utmost diligence to measure every one of their parts ...*
>
> *I have very frequently travelled not only in different parts of Italy but also out of it, that I might entirely, from them, comprehend what the whole had been and reduce it into design.*
> Andrea Palladio, Preface to *The Four Books of Architecture*, 1570

> *The object of the present publication has been to furnish ... such a view of the principles of architecture, more particularly that of the British Isles, [to] afford the guardians of ecclesiastical edifices such clear discriminative remarks on the buildings now existing, as may enable them to judge with considerable accuracy of restorations necessary to be made in those venerable edifices that are under their peculiar care.*
> Thomas Rickman, *An Attempt to Discriminate the Styles of Architecture*, 1817

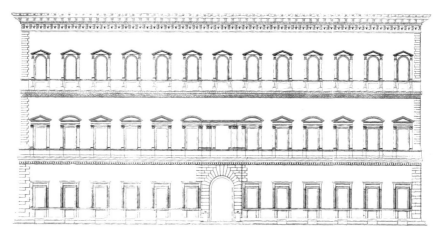

4.9 Architectural exemplars have been valued in all ages. The accurately drawn records in Letarouilly's *Edifices of Modern Rome* were a prime source for Italianate architecture of the nineteenth century.

4.10 (above) Buildings which mark important technological advances or become symbols of a particular architectural movements are likely to achieve the status of monuments once their significance is recognised. The iron bridge at Coalbrookdale (Abraham Darby 1778) was the first structure of its kind in the world.

4.11 (right) The Flatiron Building in New York City (D H Burnham & Co 1902) was the city's first skyscraper meriting the name. It was a favourite subject for picture postcards. This one records the way in which it was framed and clad, matters of great curiosity at the time.

Active preservation of entire buildings on this account was not at first the rule and it was generally accepted (though not completely without misgiving) that an ancient building like the Colosseum could be simultaneously an immensely valuable architectural specimen and a convenient source of building materials. Even the revered Pantheon had the bronze girders of its portico looted for the creation of Bernini's baldacchino for St Peter's basilica; but from about the beginning of the fifteenth century, when Brunelleschi and Donatello were busy among the ruins of Rome measuring columns and entablatures, the unique importance of old buildings as exemplars and embodiments of architectural knowledge (architectural truth to the Renaissance mind) began to be matters of earnest discussion.

Many architects today are too sensitive to the charge of being backward-looking or of being found guilty of 'copying' to draw heavily on the accumulated architectural experience of the past, but the preservation of good textbook examples as visible evidence of stages in architectural development is still one of the best understood and most generally accepted reasons for preservation.

Pleasing and picturesque

Scholarly study of old buildings was, in fact, for long limited to classical remains. Gothic buildings were not accorded systematic examination or treated as exemplars until well into the nineteenth century, but they established some claim for preservation during the eighteenth century, when reaction against artificiality and materialism often went hand in hand with an admiration for the Gothic and a romantic attitude to ruins.

> *Ruins move lively and pleasing reflections ... on the persons who have inhabited them [and] with yews and hollies, in a wild thicket ...*
> *make one of the most agreeable objects that the best of landscape painters can invent.*
> Sir John Vanbrugh, 1709

> *I think the Ruin a great Addition to the Beauty of the Lake. There is something vastly picturesque and pleasing to the Imagination in such Objects, that they are a great Addition to every Landskip.*
> William Gilpin, 1748

The feelings involved were essentially subjective, with ruins evoking thoughts of an idealised mediaeval past, but in England and Wales this early, unscholarly attitude to the 'Gothick' was happily associated with the development of landscape design. Ruins, in particular, were preserved (even, at times, newly built) as picturesque objects, to beautify a view and endow a landscape with a pleasing flavour of antiquity.

The landscape movement has a special significance in the context of this study, in that it demonstrated that preservation (in the terms then understood) could be a creative act, exploiting the visual qualities of an old building in a designed setting.

The history of architectural scholarship in relation to the practice of architecture is a matter for separate study, but we will have to return later to one important consequence of the Gothic Revival – the practice of 'restoration', referred to in the quotation from Rickman (page 21) and the related philosophical debate over the treatment of genuine historical relics.

The impulse to preserve

It is clear that civilised communities have been concerned to preserve monuments of their own past for well over a thousand years. The motives for preservation have been, in varying degrees, pride, aesthetic pleasure, reverence and curiosity.

In this context, I find in John Gwynn's *London and Westminster Improved*, one of the most compelling and dramatic statements of this impulse to preserve. Look again at the passage (quoted on page 15) about Henry the Seventh's chapel in Westminster Abbey. Here we have a thoughtful, innovative thinker, writing not about the past but about the radical replanning of London. In his book he proposes the creation of a completely new main road system and yet he speaks to us across more than two centuries with the voice of a committed conservator. A majority of his planning proposals were eventually put into effect, some of them as late as the 1950s and invariably with great practical benefit to London, but rarely with the sensitive eye to 'publick magnificence' shown by Gwynn in 1766.

In one brief paragraph Gwynn rolls up a whole philosophy of conservation. Consider the implications of his words. First, he identifies the chapel as an inherited national treasure, an extraordinary work of art which should not be left to fall apart. It is a rare monument, an 'extremely fine (and) exquisite… model of Gothick architecture', an exemplar of such importance that every little detail should be safeguarded. The messages it brings from the past should not be allowed to become garbled. 'Not an ornament or single member should suffer the least alteration' he says, but, having regard to its already decayed condition, 'it ought to be repaired before it is too late'. This could almost be William Morris, writing on SPAB (Society for the Protection of Ancient Buildings) headed paper more than a century later.

Further, the idea of 'a case for the whole to prevent all further injuries', extreme as it may sound, vividly embodies the idea of *custodianship*, dear to the SPAB and the rock on which all modern conservation philosophies are founded.

4.12a Gravesend. Architectural oddities, follies and freaks stake an easy claim for preservation. The more recent they are in date, however, the less likely they are to be recognised. This shopfront was destroyed before it was even considered for listing. The preservation of such historical eccentricities can, of course, present special difficulties, if they are not to become unusable relics. However, despite its seemingly over-specialised design this shop front could have served a number of different businesses not requiring large window displays.

4.12b High Holborn, London. For this shopfront, by contrast, it is difficult to imagine a changed use which would not result in the serious erosion of its unique character.

CHAPTER 5

The Growing Popularity
of Preservation

*In all constitutional countries … public opinion prepares the way for
legislation. No Acts for the defence of monuments can be passed and
no funds voted … unless there be in the background in the mind of
the people a certain force of intelligent belief in the need for an agency
of the kind … Public opinion, when left to itself, is in its very nature
an unbalanced force, acting spasmodically upon the stimulus supplied
by some striking event … What is required is some permanent agency
representing the public mind at its best and always kept in working
order.*
G Baldwin Brown, *The Care of Ancient Monuments*, 1905

The rise of preservation and amenity societies

The classes of preservable buildings so far described were all attracting
varying degrees of reverence and even action to preserve (for example, by
the Society of Antiquaries) long before the middle of the nineteenth century and long before Britain, at least, had effective preservation laws.
Tracing the progress, step by step, of the ways in which public opinion in
these matters has been organised, coherent conservation philosophies
evolved and legislative controls imposed, is very largely a matter of tracing
the history of the organisations dedicated to building preservation. Their
story is one of ever-widening interest in the relics of the past in which their
range of vision extended beyond an initial handful of universally acknowledged, precious monuments to include a host of lesser and later buildings
of historic interest.

The genesis of the first of these organisations (in Britain, that is), the Society for the Protection of Ancient Buildings (SPAB), is considered later but it should be noted at this point that that Society, although deriving its authority from a core of expert founding members, was conceived in a surge of emotional reaction against what was seen as ignorant destruction. This is the way all such movements begin. The dismissive remark often heard from those who wish to justify the demolition of an historic building today, that the desire to preserve it stems from 'mere sentiment', can itself be dismissed. If we are not preserving buildings because they have the power to stir a whole variety of emotions, we are engaged in a sterile activity reserved for scholars alone. In this connection, the quotation from Baldwin Brown above is as relevant today as it was in 1905.

The Society for the Protection of Ancient Buildings said at the time of its formation, in 1877, that it was concerned with 'buildings of all times and styles', but it was inescapably the child of its time. The original members would have had difficulty in recognising a 'modern' building (Georgian, let alone Victorian) as being worthy of their concern. Frontiers of perception, as to what is of value, are invariably pushed forward by a party within an existing group – a fact demonstrated by the emergence of the Georgian Group (from the SPAB) in 1937. As an inevitable progress, the Victorian Society (1958) and, more recently, the Twentieth Century Society have come into existence. The latter is achieving the same status as its predecessors by being recognised as the 'official' advocate for later buildings. The skill and expertise of these societies has frequently been underpinned – and this calls for no apology – by public anger over the loss of such buildings as the Adelphi, the Euston Arch, the Coal Exchange and the Firestone Factory.

Some societies have tended to concentrate on – or have been formed to safeguard – particular building types. The names of the Association for Industrial Archaeology, the Wind and Watermill section of the SPAB, the Cinema Theatre Association and the Theatres Trust (actually a statutory body, rather than a society) explain their purposes. The Ancient Monuments Society, founded in 1924 to study and conserve historic buildings and examples of fine craftsmanship, has given particular attention to redundant churches. SAVE Britain's Heritage has taken to itself the special task of campaigning for improvements in public provision for conservation as well as spearheading the preservation of endangered buildings and places.

Evidence of a broader, relatively unspecialised interest in building conservation can be seen in the host of local preservation groups, preservation trusts and amenity societies which have come into existence since the 1960s. Many of these are concerned with defending the character of their own neighbourhood, rather than with relics of a particular kind or quality.

The need to see evidence of the past: the non-monumental monument

... If we do not take steps to protect and preserve buildings of value, either in their own right or because of the contribution they make to a pleasant townscape or village scene, they may well be lost and, once lost, they cannot be replaced ... It is better that old buildings are not set apart but are woven into the fabric of the living and working community. Public opinion is now overwhelmingly in favour of conserving and enhancing the familiar and cherished local scene and authorities should take account of this ...
Department of the Environment, *Circular 8/87*, March 1987 (Introduction)

The tendency, almost world-wide, in the years since World War II has been toward intensification of general (that is, unspecialised) public interest in the preservation of old buildings or, more recently, in what is called 'the built environment'. This has been accompanied by a broadening of the spectrum of buildings considered worthy of preservation. The reasons for these trends are complex and worthy of detailed examination but we need only note the consequences.

The idea of the precious monument, preservable in isolation, remains firmly rooted but no longer completely satisfies a widespread public desire to see evidence of the past in the familiar scene. Quite modest buildings, some of them of relatively recent origin, now excite admiration and affection and also attract scholarly attention.

'New' movements are usually not altogether new. The instructions given to the official investigators as they set about listing historic buildings after the 1944 and 1947 Town and Country Planning Acts and after the destruction of whole city areas in World War II (see Appendix 6) were remarkably forward-looking, laying the foundation for wider-ranging protection than had at that time been contemplated in most other countries. The steady development of this inclusive tendency was heavily counterbalanced by a marked official reluctance in earlier years to speed the process of listing or make the protective processes really effective. Also, in contrast to the situation in, say, France, little more than symbolic public funding was directed to preservation. The enlightened spirit of the first

5.1 Public interest in preserving the visible evidence of the past has sharpened considerably since the 1960s. The preservation of isolated, exceptional buildings, deprived of context and meaning, is now likely to be criticised rather than applauded. There is, today, an expectation that the character and nature of a place will be respected as a whole and that there will continue to be a variety of buildings speaking of the social, economic and leisure life of the community. This corner patisserie is, in this sense, as valuable as the grand hotels in the Paris Marais.

5.2a Shad Thames, Bermondsey. A street of riverside warehouses is, in the eyes of many people, a more significant document of the history of Bermondsey than the fragments of its mediaeval abbey, but the effective preservation of such buildings when the river trade has gone can be problematical. The buildings only seemed truly complete when they were alive with noisy and dangerous activity at all levels on both wharfside and roadside.

5.2b The same street today is active in a completely different, wholly non-industrial way. The surviving buildings are well cared for but their meaning has been unavoidably eroded. In some particulars, the devices employed in revival might be described as evocation, rather than conservation. For example, the ornamental brackets under some of the new (or renewed) bridges are hanging from, rather than supporting the structure! This kind of commercially powered recycling has been described as 'going for the least undesirable option' since the alternative could well have been the total loss of an historically important group.

5.3 (right) Upminster Mill.
The passage of time can alter
perceptions of what should be
protected and preserved. Once
common building types, like
windmills, have become rare
and treasured objects.

5.4 (below) Manchester.
This old terra-cotta cinema
front is much more than a
pleasing architectural incident
in the street. It is a tangible
record of the life and leisure
of ordinary people in the
early decades of the twentieth
century.

booklet of *Instructions to Investigators* was, nevertheless, historically
significant, in preparing the ground for (not, at that stage, seeing provision
made for) what has come to be called 'area conservation'.

We should now take note of the kinds of buildings – often quite
unmonumental in architectural character – which came to be considered
as worthy of protection alongside the major monuments and antiquities
already highlighted. The italicised words in the following paragraph are
lifted from or paraphrase the post-War *Instructions*.

Exceptional buildings which incorporated some *architectural or structural innovation* obviously had a claim for preservation as documents of

the past, as did *architectural freaks and follies*, but in an age which had seen (and continues to see) more rapid, if not more extensive, destruction than had hitherto been experienced, buildings which were good representatives of an historically significant kind, *possessing the characteristic virtues of the school of design which produced them*, also came to be highly regarded. The grand Georgian mansion attributable to a well-known architect and the contemporary terrace of houses run up by a local carpenter using a pattern book both came to be valued. The latter represented civilised qualities of urban design in which the individual units were less important than the totality. Reminders of the history of *agriculture* and *industry* were also considered – not only the great monuments of technology (like the train-sheds at Kings Cross and St Pancras or, more recently, the airship hangars at Cardington) but also relatively common or once common objects like windmills, barns and pumping stations. Consideration also began to be given to buildings, which were not readily classified, which were not the products of one historical period or the creations of a single creative mind but which were interesting and pleasing as the result of a visibly evidenced process of *historical change and accretion*. Finally, the *group value* of relatively modest buildings was noted.

The effectiveness or otherwise of the resulting inventory and the system of protection which accompanied it are matters for separate study. Here we are concerned with the desire to preserve and this brings us to the question of how public opinion operates in this area.

New battlegrounds

We started this chapter with the idea that, throughout history, certain monumental buildings have been marked out for preservation in some sense from the moment of their completion. For a variety of reasons other kinds of building, not necessarily monumental in the architectural sense, have also commended themselves for protection. These kinds have all been in some way special, but rarity and artistic quality have clearly not been the only tests.

In very recent times, preservation has moved from a situation in which the identification of what was special was largely the province of scholars to one in which public opinion is marking out new battlegrounds. Most readers will be able to think of cases in their own experience where energetic local high street campaigns have been fought to prevent the destruction of what historians and other experts have dismissed as unexceptional buildings.

Whatever case there may be for correcting misinformation and improving the level of general education in these matters (this, incidentally, is one responsibility that experts tend to neglect), it is a grave mistake to brush aside these expressions of very real public awareness and concern. The expert who says, 'But there are far better buildings to worry about than these', deserves the sharp rejoinder, 'Not here there aren't!'

Growing demand for the conservation of what has been called 'the familiar and cherished local scene' has focused attention on whole families of lesser buildings with undeniable qualities, well worthy of care and attention. Unfortunately, if the buildings themselves are not singled out for statutory protection, the available controls – and the determination of the controllers – may prove inadequate to prevent architectural erosion.

5.5a (above right) An estate of factory workers' cottages, sensitively designed in 'village' groupings with good quality traditional materials and careful detailing in vernacular style.

5.5b (below right) 'Progress' Estate, Well Hall, Eltham. Cottages on the same estate made indistinguishable from speculative buildings by the substitution of mass-produced windows and fences. Others have had their hand-made clay roof tiles replaced by factory-made tiles. In some places the total effect of the changes has been so radical as to erase all memory of the qualities which first made the place seem special.

The extent and nature of public concern are matters of fundamental importance. In looking at the philosophical background to the duties of the preserver we must not lose sight of the fact that authority to interfere with the rights of private ownership derives from an informed consensus that preservation is in the public interest. Experts are needed to provide historical and technical know-how in order to make sensible decisions about what should be done but, ultimately, non-expert opinion determines how much can be done.

> *As more buildings are listed and conservation areas designated, more people are likely to become involved ... Their experience ... will doubtless colour their view of conservation.*
> Department of the Environment *Circular 8/87*

> *Historic preservation has been traditionally characterised as 'elitist', but this viewpoint is being modified as wider sections of the population begin to understand the cultural values of their own habitat and to demand a role in the formulation of plans for its preservation. This development should by no means be regarded as undesirable (even if it poses new and not always easy problems for the professional). To the contrary, it presents an unparalleled opportunity to correct some of the sense of alienation which is so characteristic of modern society. It affords the opportunity for the citizens to regain a sense of identity with their own origins of which they have often been robbed by the sheer process of urbanisation.*
> James Marston Fitch, *Historic Preservation*, 1990 edition

This brings us back, for a moment, to the question of national and local societies concerned with preservation. The 'grass roots' movement has been guided and informed by the Civic Trust, founded in 1957 to 'promote higher standards of architecture and civic planning in Britain and encourage a wider interest in the appearance of our towns and villages'. The Civic Amenities Act of 1967, which introduced to Britain the concept of 'conservation areas' to reinforce and extend the existing protective legislation, was a milestone in the life of the Trust. It also signalled a new and broader public awareness of what was at risk.

Guarding resources: 'green' issues

From about the 1960s there was undoubtedly an undercurrent of fear of the new in 'grassroots' conservation campaigns, often arising from justified disillusionment with post-war renewal. New development was frequently greeted with mistrust rather than expectation, whilst the most humdrum existing buildings were defended as if they were irreplaceable. More recently, however, a less anxious, more reasoned 'green' motive has become apparent.

> One valid case for preservation is economic. Can we afford to rebuild the environment every generation? … New construction is pricing itself out of many markets, making recycling not a sentimental exercise but a necessity. Another case for preservation is energy: important in the decision to recycle instead of rebuild. The residual value of energy built into old cities is enormous … Energy is wasted when any old building is pulled down.
> Harry M Weese, 1976, quoted by James Marston Fitch in *Historic Preservation*, 1990 edition

> Keeping in touch with the past and preserving the best for [future generations] is not an optional extra, especially at a time in history when we have an unprecedented capacity to change and destroy what has gone before … The central idea of sustainability is that we should achieve an acceptable quality of life, where necessary through growth, without disinheriting our grandchildren or mortgaging their future.
> English Heritage, *Sustaining the Historic Environment: new perspectives on the future*, 1997

> If sustainability means anything at all, our mentality has to change. The energy taken to produce eight bricks is equivalent to a barrel of oil, so every time we knock down a building there are big energy implications. We need a mindset where we think carefully before we knock things down and don't always blame the buildings for problems.
> Michael Coupe, Head of Planning, English Heritage, 2002

> In 1972 we were consuming the earth's resources at less than the rate at which the world could reproduce them. We are now consuming the earth's resources at three times the rate at which it can reproduce them … We are heading rapidly for bankruptcy. We have no option. We have to change.
> Peter Fall, RICS President, 2002

5.6 Reasoned arguments for sustainable growth, designed to avoid mortgaging the future for the sake of short term gain, have led to renewed examination of conservation policies of all kinds. Retaining and adapting, rather than replacing old buildings, is now seen as a sensible safeguarding of past investments of energy; desirable economically, as well as environmentally. If sustainability is to be more than a 'buzz word', however, there needs to be a fundamental and general change of attitude toward waste. The more popular, but, in the end, relatively painless operation of building conservation controls can only ever be a first step on a hard road.

The idea is gaining currency that old buildings, even of modest architectural quality, represent a past investment of energy and materials, the care and sensible use of which can eliminate unnecessary new assaults on the earth's resources. It has also been observed that many traditionally constructed buildings have served a series of uses over a very long period, whilst the demolition and replacement of office and residential blocks which, after only 30 years, have 'reached the end of their economic life' is a fairly common sight. This is not an argument against modern design or construction methods, but it is an indication that older buildings, with their short spans, relatively small elements of construction and record of adaptability, may yet have a great deal to offer to modern life.

The wastage of readily adaptable buildings has been aggravated in the relatively recent past by what has been called 'the bad building syndrome', that is, the scapegoating of buildings for completely unrelated ills. This may be observed daily when politicians and journalists refer to 'crumbling old Victorian schools' (or whatever) needing to be torn down and replaced. In many cases the buildings are actually well built and capable of further long and useful life. The questions needing to be asked are 'Who let the buildings get into this state?' and 'Will total renewal really end the cycle of neglect that is the fundamental cause of present dissatisfaction?'

The 'bad wicked building' notion was embedded solidly into public housing legislation and its financial provisions for most of the twentieth century. Houses that failed the tests of age (why age?), which were in poor condition and lacking in basic facilities were condemned as slums, cleared away and their sites redeveloped. The social effects of clear-fell policies are much criticised today but, for the purposes of this study, one point only needs to be noted. A number of areas that, for whatever reason, escaped the clearance process have survived to become desirable residential neigh-bourhoods in which the former slums change hands at astronomical prices. Age, in such cases, has become a merit, rather than a defect, whilst poor conditions and lack of basic facilities have been dealt with in the obvi-ous way, by investment. Clearly, it was not the houses that were at fault in these cases, but it has always been a great deal easier to blame the buildings than to investigate and deal with the root causes of social stress. It may be noted in passing that, when 'gentrification' occurs, it is not only the individual houses, but the whole infrastructure that magically improves. An economically-aware and articulate population does not tolerate muni-cipal neglect.

The modern exploitation of traditional buildings has, nevertheless, not always played to their strengths. Appropriately maintained and sensibly occupied they will usually adapt to reasonable requirements of utility and comfort, but their nature must be understood. It is obvious that overload-ing of floors, for example, will cause serious problems, but there are more subtle risks. The use of hard, impervious materials in the belief that they are, by definition, better than the old, weak and porous fabric they replace, can seriously interfere with a traditionally constructed building's ability to 'breathe' naturally. Cement rich pointing and dense render coatings may

seem to give an assurance of resistance to damp penetration but, by form-
ing impenetrable barriers they are likely to upset a virtuous rhythm of
absorption and drying out, leading eventually to serious physical damage.
The modern passion for restricting all air movement by sealing every com-
partment and every roof space can also lead to problems for a building
(and, often enough, for its occupants) which would not be experienced
with natural ventilation. If, at the same time, interiors are, quite unnecessarily, heated to American office standards, there is also likely to be movement in joinery and in wood structural members. The resulting faults and
discomforts will invariably be blamed on the building, whilst the remedies
employed – introducing further alien forms of rigid construction to
'strengthen' the old fabric – may lead to yet further trouble, which again
will be put down to the unsatisfactory nature of the building rather than
the ignorance of the practitioner.

There is a broader economic as well as a practical point here. Old,
'traditional' buildings (not in this context, limited to protected historic
buildings) account for not less than 25 per cent of our building stock. If
they are treated with knowledge and care, the materials and crafts required
for their maintenance are likely to remain available. If the assumption is
made that all new methods and materials are superior to the old, the old
will fade out of existence and it will steadily become more difficult and
expensive to sustain an economically important inheritance.

The innocent might suppose that modern, efficient industries would
inevitably adapt to meet such a manifest need. The reverse tendency has, in
fact, been observable, with old buildings having to adapt themselves to a
range of goods and materials designed for highly centralised production
methods and high pressure salesmanship. To take only one example, the
heavy concrete interlocking tile has replaced slate on hundreds of thousands, possibly millions, of old buildings. The substitute does, of course,
have some advantages. Unlike slates, these tiles can be produced cheaply by
factory workers and laid by the barely skilled.

Sustainability has become something of a cliché, but it is a vital consideration here. Resources of all kinds that have come down to us should be
treated with a sense of responsibility toward coming generations. We
should not waste our inherited wealth or deprive our successors of the
choices that we have enjoyed. We should also be vigilant in monitoring
external trends that operate to narrow those choices.

Guarding the evidence

When all practical, economic and emotional reasons for preserving buildings have been given due weight, conservation professionals, that is, conservation planners, historians, crafts people and those who exercise
statutory controls, as well as architects, surveyors and engineers specifying
works, bear a particular responsibility. Individually or as members of a
team, they have the key task of holding intact, so far as they can, a body
of evidence from the past. The preservation of historic buildings does not,
in fact, make much sense if it does not achieve so much. But it should by
now be clear that this simple prescription raises more questions than it
answers. As we have seen, not only do the buildings now presented for
preservation cross a very wide spectrum indeed, but so do the motives for
preserving them and (we have yet to consider this) the circumstances surrounding them.

It is permissible to wonder how any one philosophy can be devised to
serve the demands of, say, essential repairs to a Saxon church or adaptive
works to a listed 1930s cinema – or the preservation of a much loved townscape in which no single element is, in itself, of outstanding interest.
This question will crop up from time to time throughout the following
chapters, but the reader will do well to keep constantly in view the
title of the first chapter. Philosophy provides guiding lights – not instant
prescriptions.

PART III

Means and Manner of Preservation

CHAPTER *6*

Control by Legal Process

*All too often, (people) have created legislation to protect their
landmarks after suffering irreparable loss ... The demolition of
Pennsylvania Station in New York City was one of the events that
helped to bring about the formation of the City Landmarks
Commission. As this splendid example of the classical style was being
leveled, many architects and other concerned citizens who were trying
desperately to save it were astounded to discover that they had no
legal means of doing so.*
James Biddle and Thomas P F Hoving,
Preface to *The Rise of an American Architecture*, 1970

*When a building has survived its original functional usefulness – but
first let us be quite sure that it has ... then there are three grounds,
and only three, on which we are logically entitled to press for its
preservation: of its own intrinsic merit, of pietas, of its scenic
usefulness.*

*Of these it is the first upon which agreement is most difficult to reach.
For no yardstick of aesthetic judgment is of universal validity ... No
educated person would today contemplate the destruction of Chartres
with equanimity, but in the eighteenth century many would have
regarded it as a welcome deliverance too long delayed. And can we be
certain that the obvious necessity for preserving the temple of Paestum
would be self-evident to one brought up in the shadow of Angkor Vat?*

*Let us always beware of the uncertainty of private judgment,
remembering that what to us may be without merit may well prove to
posterity, who can view it in perspective, of considerable value.*
Osbert Lancaster, 'What Should We Preserve?' in *The Future of the Past*, 1976

*Americans rightly believe that an historic building that is threatened
with demolition is more important, at that instant, than all the rest of
the heritage put together. Our Grade I, II and II* system, they say, is a
bureaucrat's tool of convenience for doling out meagre funds to those
that have rather than to those who are in need.*

John Fidler, 'Conservation in North America', in *Building Conservation*
(periodical), September 1980

Custodianship and control

Conservation philosophy is largely concerned with practice – determining
precisely how historic buildings should be treated by the practitioner – but
it will be clear from the last chapter that any system of statutory protection
must also, by its very nature, embody contemporary philosophical attitudes. To take only one example, effective protection invariably depends on
the creation of an inventory, a list of what is to be protected – and priorities for listing are determined by a philosophy, explicit or implicit.

The underlying idea in practically all efforts to preserve old buildings,
whether by personal action or by the operation of protective laws is, as we
have already remarked, that of custodianship – a sense that we are responsible to future generations and should hand on those riches we have ourselves inherited and enjoyed. Every generation is free to neglect or destroy
its inheritance. One of the marks of a civilised people is a desire to safeguard and add to its architectural and artistic wealth.

Custodianship, in this context, is a social concept which goes beyond
the personal pleasures and private responsibilities of an owner. It implies,
in fact, the existence of Baldwin Brown's 'force of intelligent belief ... in the
mind of the people' that some buildings need to be given special protection
by limiting the rights of private owners to do as they please with their own
property. The quotation from Osbert Lancaster at the head of this chapter
warns us that underlying social attitudes and priorities may vary quite
widely from time to time and from place to place, but the custodianship
principle, once accepted, places a particular burden on expert advisers at
every level to look to the interests of posterity as well as those of the present time and to attempt to educate 'the mind of the people' accordingly.

A glance at the Chronology (Appendix 1) will quickly destroy the myth
(at least so far as it relates to building preservation) that the British have
always been distinguished by an obsessive concern with the past. Britain
was neither the first nor the most determined of legislators in the field of
preservation. The idea of protection by law has, nevertheless, been around

in Europe for a long time. We need to look at some earlier attempts at the framing of control systems for the light that they will throw on attitudes to building preservation.

Imposed restraints, expressed in special laws, have varied in their scope and force according to the political and other circumstances which produced them. Few national statutes have been quite so uncompromising as the first Greek monument law:

> *All objects of antiquity in Greece, as the productions of the ancestors*
> *of the Hellenic people, are regarded as the common national*
> *possession of all Hellenes.*
> Monument Act, Kingdom of Greece, 1834 (*Article 61*)

One of the very earliest of modern preservation statutes, however, was framed some years earlier by Grand Duke Ludwig for the state of Hesse-Darmstadt in 1818.

Hesse and France

To many readers the reference to Hesse-Darmstadt will sound impossibly obscure but, in fact, the brief Hesse law contained nearly all the elements found in modern legislation. In the preamble it referred to surviving monuments of architecture as being 'among the most important and interesting evidences of history [whose] preservation is greatly to be wished'. The first Article charged the State's Higher College of Building with creating a 'correct inventory' of buildings worthy of preservation 'on historical or artistic grounds' and required prior approval to be obtained before any building in this inventory could be altered or demolished. It has to be added, however, that really detailed inventorisation did not begin in Hesse until 1870.

The first moves for the formal protection of monuments have commonly been made as a reaction to some traumatic act of destruction. As early as 1815, the great German architect, Karl Friedrich Schinkel (1781–1841), had reported to the Prussian government on the damage to mediaeval buildings which had occurred in the French wars. Schinkel set the basic pattern not only for Prussian protective legislation and state decrees (49 of them, including Hesse's) but also for virtually all subsequent laws elsewhere. He recommended the appointment of officers concerned with monument care and proposed the preparation of a state inventory of buildings and movable art works of dates earlier than the middle of the seventeenth century.

France must nevertheless be granted precedence as the first country to create an adequately staffed and financed official preservation agency to carry its laws into effect. In many respects it still retains the leadership it established in the second quarter of the nineteenth century.

In France the first surge of reaction followed the shock of the French Revolution, which had as one of its declared purposes the destruction of the memory of feudalism and despotic rule. The major shift of educated opinion, however, occurred in 1811 under the First Empire when the supreme monument of the Romanesque, the Abbey of Cluny, was demolished.

After the July Revolution of 1830, the new Minister of Instruction appointed a General Inspector of Historical Monuments. The second holder of this post was Prosper Mérimée (1803–1870), an inspired organ-iser (and, as it happens, the author of *Carmen*). In 1837 a *Commission des Monuments Historiques* with supporting committees was set up to start the work of inventorisation and restoration of monuments. When a compre-hensive Monument Act eventually passed into law in 1887, it left the administrative and scholarly structures of the 1837 Commission intact, simply codifying a situation which had, by then, existed for fifty years.

The creation of an agency with both expertise and state funds set in train an immense programme of monument restoration and fuelled a philosophical controversy which raged throughout the century. The rever-berations of this debate are still felt today and the issues will be examined in the next chapter. For the time being it is necessary only to note the his-torical climate in which French legislation and practice developed.

Control in Britain

Is it too much to hope that Sir John Lubbock's modest measure for the preservation of our national monuments will escape shipwreck?

Seventy-seven monuments, including over twenty stone circles are enumerated … The number, when antiquaries are fairly on the search will probably be more than doubled. The proposal is certainly not a whit too soon.
Graphic (periodical) 15 March 1873

One feels a sentimental regret that Sir John Lubbock's Bill was rejected by the House of Commons. But closer examination shows pretty clearly that even Druidical and Roman ruins may be bought at

*too dear a price. (The Bill proposed) such extensive powers as to
paralyse free enterprise in many directions. If a man digging the
foundation for a new house came on a Roman pavement his
operations might be postponed sine die... The tyranny and
interference would become intolerable ... Anything in the shape of an
'antiquity' would become hateful to the sight ...*

*Altogether our old monuments are as safe under their present
custodians as they are likely to be under any others.*
Graphic (periodical) 18 April 1874

In Britain, progress was slower and more painful than in France. It took
nine years, from the first unsuccessful Bill in 1873–4, for any kind of protective law to find its way on to the statute book. The Ancient Monuments
Protection Act (an enfeebled version of an intelligently drafted bill of 1880)
was eventually passed into law in 1882. Compared with what was happening across the Channel, it represented a late, extremely tentative and visibly
reluctant essay in control. The Act gave slight protection to no more than
68 monuments of great antiquity in the whole of Britain (there were 2,000
monuments classés in France by 1887) and, in deference to those who were
determined to resist any monuments law as a gross interference with the
sacred rights of private ownership, it contained no powers of compulsion
against owners. It did, however, provide for monuments to be taken into
guardianship or acquired by agreement by the Commissioners of Works,
following which, preservation could be undertaken at public expense on
the advice of Inspectors of Ancient Monuments. Nevertheless significant
action, even on so limited a front, was barely visible for the next quarter of
a century.

The ways in which the British laws developed and, step by dragging
step, were given teeth after 1882, can be studied in detail elsewhere (but see
Appendices 1 and 8). In brief, progress over the first half of the twentieth
century took the form of giving more effective control over what were
termed ancient monuments (predominantly roofless mediaeval, Roman
and prehistoric remains). During the post-World War II period additional
controls were built into the planning legislation to protect a far wider variety of buildings of special architectural or historic interest, mostly post-
mediaeval, the majority of them being of late seventeenth-century or later
dates and in modern beneficial use.

So far as inventories are concerned, the first for Britain was the brief list
of monuments included on the Schedule to the 1882 Act (hence, 'scheduled

monument' – a term still in use). 'Statutory lists' of buildings of special architectural or historic interest were put in hand after the 1944 and 1947 Town and Country Planning Acts. The principles laid down for the investigators who produced the first statutory lists have already been touched on above.

Both sets of lists – of monuments and historic buildings – still have a separate existence and are under constant revision. The division, peculiar to Britain, is in itself a matter of history rather than practical necessity. A philosophical basis – the idea that 'ancient monuments' call for a different degree of care from 'historic buildings' – is not easy to argue. Clearly, the preservation of a Roman fort or a ruined abbey must call for different kinds of expertise from those needed in dealing with a seventeenth-century mansion or an iron-framed Victorian commercial building, but the degree of care required is not necessarily greater in the former case. The 'bite' of the legal sanctions should be the same across the board; the manner and stringency with which the controls are operated in individual cases need be determined only when the machinery of control has to be brought into motion.

If the two systems are ever united by new legislation the only unarguably desirable division will be between those historic structures, of whatever age, which are demonstrably capable and those which are quite clearly incapable of some kind of modern beneficial use. Even here, the only fundamental difference required would be in the provisions dealing with financial matters (primarily compensation) and with acquisition or custodianship of privately owned buildings by the official agencies.

Statutory control philosophy and practice

It will be apparent to the reader that workable preservation laws require certain basic provisions:

- A definition of what is to be preserved, usually in the form of a list.
- A method by which the controlling authorities will be alerted to possible danger (commonly, a requirement for a notice or an application before a protected building can be demolished or altered).
- A way of permitting harmless or desirable works to proceed following negotiation with the authority's experts (a consent or certificate, usually carrying conditions).
- Effective sanctions against offenders (fines, imprisonment, enforced reinstatement, direct action to repair, expropriation).

Other provisions to meet special needs, such as grants toward the cost of unusually expensive repairs and arrangements for voluntary transfer of custodianship are also often present in modern legislation, but the above four elements are essential if control is to work at all.

Marked differences in philosophical attitudes underlying superficially similar national laws are to be observed principally in the range of their inventories, the stringency of their sanctions and the extent of their financial provisions.

The British system, for example, protects a large number and wide range of buildings and can be effective in preventing or limiting damage. It is not ideally designed for the promotion of conservation initiatives. It provides relatively little in the way of financial incentives, being based firmly on the assumption that, since most of the buildings are not of great antiquity and are perfectly capable of earning their keep in a modern world, the responsibility for care should rest almost entirely with their owners. Building owners may be inconvenienced if they turn to unskilled advisers or attempt to carry out works without professional help and are then unable to steer their proposals through the official obstacle course, but they are not actually required to employ experts.

The position is much the same on the official side. Although the operation of the controls is left largely to district planning authorities, they are not required to employ specialist staff; and those who do, rarely assign them to senior positions in their planning departments. Here again, the philosophy informing the legislators seems to have been that the general run of preservation work is not particularly demanding. In the more important cases the expertise of national agencies like English Heritage will – or so it is assumed – be brought into play. The controlling local authorities themselves (I am tempted to say 'as a result') vary widely in performance. Few of them see building conservation as a major responsibility and some take virtually no interest in it at all (see Appendix 8). Even the most committed make relatively little use of (for example) emergency repairs powers. Prosecutions for illegal works are uncommon and the central agencies rarely intervene where local authorities have failed to act.

The French system is, by comparison, highly centralised. Their inventory is more selective, ignoring altogether some buildings, which would be highly valued in Britain. Those buildings which are given full protection, however, are rigorously controlled. There is an assumption – built into their legislative apparatus for so long that it is no longer seen as requiring explanation or justification – that no building owner can be trusted to carry out works to a protected monument other than under the superintendence of state-certified specialist architects. By this means, virtually all significant works to major monuments (not only those in government ownership) are effectively under the direct control of a government agency and approved conservation works are, as a matter of general expectation, well funded by subvention. The environs of important monuments are also closely and consistently protected.

The other side of this coin is that it is difficult to persuade a French monuments expert that one is serious in suggesting that, say, a late nineteenth-century theatre or *hôtel de ville* is worthy of protection in its own right. Although the French were early in the field with legislation for 'area conservation' as well as monument preservation, they tend to believe that the ordinary 'flesh and bones' of the town can be left to look after itself. In the vicinity of national monuments the ensemble will, in any case, be well tended and in many provincial towns development pressures have been so subdued as to make official complacency (in our terms) seem justified.

North American experience contrasts sharply with both Britain and France. In the USA there is no comprehensive nationwide system of 'landmark' protection. Each state's legislation is separately framed, but all within a philosophical framework set by the United States constitution, which in general protects the right of Americans to do as they please with their own property. Some places have had sophisticated and very effective protection laws for many years (like Charlestown and New Orleans, for example, since the 1930s), but every stage of protection is open to challenge on constitutional, if no other, grounds. This includes the inventorisation or 'registration' process itself.

The USA, nevertheless, has typically tended to offer better incentives for voluntary conservation. The inalienable right to develop land to its full potential within defined 'zoning' limits can, to a limited extent and in some places, be transferred to a neighbouring site (by sale of 'air rights') with the approval of the local administration. The authority can then impose a 'preservation easement' on the exporting site, such an easement being enforceable under the general property laws. Another kind of incentive to companies recycling old buildings has at times produced a situation where owners actually became anxious to see comparatively modest buildings 'landmarked' in order to secure significant tax advantages.

It is tempting, in making comparisons of this kind, to identify the special virtues of each system and propose an 'ideal' model that might eventually be adopted by all. We should certainly learn from one another and, when it is practicable to do so, adopt practices that have proved to be useful elsewhere, but present differences in legal controls should not be assumed to be accidental or readily alterable. Protective laws, as we have already seen, are invariably the product of a people's history. They also sit within broader frameworks of law, which may differ fundamentally from one nation to another. To take only one example, the 'air rights', referred to above, are a reality in the USA. In British law the concept is meaningless. To adopt the idea here would involve a complete rewriting of our planning legislation together with half a century of case law. Similarly, our own protective apparatus has features American conservators envy, but which are, in practical terms, unexportable.

CHAPTER 7

The Practice of Preservation: Historical Background

Matters of choice

Whatever motives society may have for preserving old buildings and whatever legislative and other controls may be available, preservation is ultimately, in the most literal sense, in the hands of the building professionals and crafts people. The most pressing philosophical questions must, therefore, be those concerned with practice.

We have already observed that building preservation at its simplest is a matter of carrying out necessary repairs in order to maintain utility. Even when working on buildings of little or no distinction, few of us would be happy to leave evidence of our handiwork in the form of unsightly scars and patches. We continually and automatically reject some courses of action, making what are, in effect, aesthetic choices in matters where the only compulsion arises from personal pride in a job tidily done. The more sensitive we feel the building to be, the more compelling and critical are the choices.

When the work is being carried out for motives other than simple self-interest, philosophical questions at once begin to arise. If the building is seen as a precious relic, a work of art, a document of national history, an example of a rare or defunct craft or an element in a valued landscape or townscape, then everything done to it has to be viewed in this light – with a special kind of care and respect.

This moves us at once into an area where differences of judgement are likely to arise even amongst the most sensitive and best informed practitioners, since the activity itself is not amenable to hard and fast definitions and rules. The test of good maintenance is that the building is being kept in secure, weatherproof and usable condition by regular repairs carried out to a consistent pattern at reasonable cost. Different maintenance surveyors of equal competence working for the same client and in possession of all the essential facts about the circumstances of the client and the nature of the building are not likely to arrive at wildly contrasting plans of action. Confronted by the need to preserve a vulnerable structure posing complex repair problems in which cost-effectiveness – although a consideration – cannot be allowed to determine all choices, and where common maintenance techniques may be clearly inappropriate, professional unanimity will be a great deal harder to achieve.

When dealing with historic buildings that are in modern beneficial use, the most careful practitioners may differ about how competing demands are to be balanced, and they will produce quite different solutions to the same sets of problems. The attempt to formulate bedrock principles applicable to all cases (see Appendices 2–5) will continue for as long as there are experts with breath in their bodies to debate the matter, but there are no sure-fire, universally accepted tests for the conserver as there are for the maintenance surveyor.

There is, of course, a danger in making the kind of statement contained in the last sentence. It will be interpreted by some as a licence to do as they will, since (they will say) if there are no such tests, then one opinion is surely as good as another. Saying that there is no absolute truth, however, does not absolve us from being truthful. One needs only to examine a variety of projects bearing the 'preservation' or 'conservation' label to begin, quite instinctively, to range them in order – from those which achieve a satisfying standard of honesty, to those which are bad jokes, not worthy of serious consideration. It may be impossible to lay down the law but we quickly recognise the existence of a threshold beyond which inexcusable offences are being committed!

To preserve or restore

Even when we have set aside the products of blatant ignorance and commercial charlatanry, we are left with a wide spectrum of preservation activity for which, even at the extremes, some kind of justification can be constructed. In examining the different approaches to preservation which have been adopted by serious practitioners at various times, it will be instructive to look at the extremes, ranging from what we may term the strict self-denial of the archaeologist, to the unapologetic self-confidence of the creative architect.

Conflict between these extremes became explicit only at the end of the eighteenth century. It is not visible at all, for example, in Hawksmoor's advice to Dr Clarke (see the quotation on page xv). For Hawksmoor, respect for antiquity would not have excluded the recycling of old masonry in his new buildings (see Chapter 6 of Prof. Kerry Downes, *Hawksmoor*, 1969). Neither can it be detected in John Evelyn's *Dedicatory Epistle to Charles II* in 1664. Evelyn saw the decent repair and improvement of old buildings as equally desirable and natural processes which could be spoken of in the same breath and performed as one operation.

> *Your Majesty has already built and repaired more in three or four years (notwithstanding the difficulties and the necessitie of an extraordinary oeconomy for the public concernment) than all your enemies have destroyed in twenty, nay than all your Majesties predecessors have advanc'd in an hundred … [making] under the conduct of your most worthy and industrious Surveyor … useful reformations for security and delight about your Majesties Palace at Whitehall; the chargeable covering, first paving and reformation of Westminster Hall; (and) care and preparation for St Paul's, by the impiety and iniquity of the late confusions almost dilapidated …*
> John Evelyn, Dedication to the Translation of Roland Freart's *Parallel of the Ancient Architecture*, 1664

As a matter of interest, when Evelyn refers to 'your … surveyor' he is probably thinking of John Webb, the Deputy.

The later history of building preservation became fraught with conflict. By the middle of the nineteenth century there were clearly two major trends (or philosophical schools of thought) working, sometimes together, more often than not in opposition and tending to dictate opposed patterns of choice. The first directed itself toward the restoration of what was believed to be the most desirable or 'perfect' form of the building. The second (second also in point of time) was concerned with preserving intact what had been inherited from the past, by rejecting all unnecessary interventions. Although the second may be said to have triumphed to become international orthodoxy in modern times, the first resolutely refuses to die.

This brings us back to definitions and a word which, in a particular historic context, was supercharged. *Restoration*, at its most innocent, can have its simple dictionary meaning of 'the act or process of repairing … making good, reinstating'. It can also legitimately (but, in connection with historic buildings, controversially) mean 'bringing back to a former state or supposed former state'. Restoration in this special sense was at the centre of the most violent philosophical confrontation surrounding the preservation of old buildings in the nineteenth century.

Restoration: Wyatt and the cathedrals

When the cathedrals of Hereford, Durham, Salisbury and Lichfield were altered agreeably to the taste of the late Mr James Wyatt, only a few professed antiquaries dared to remonstrate … but their interference was generally treated with ridicule or resented with indignation. Salisbury and Lichfield were thought to be much improved by the demolition of their altar screens, the throwing open of the smaller chantries and the removal of ancient tombs from the graves to which they belonged, in order to range them in rank and file. These barbarisms were praised and admired because the public mind was ignorant on the subject.

Edward James Willson (in the preface to Pugin the elder's *Examples of Gothic Architecture*), 1831

One of the first signs of the coming battle royal was the conflict which led to a brilliantly creative architect, James Wyatt (1746–1813) being dubbed, not without cause, 'the Destroyer'. Wyatt's cathedral restorations in the last twelve years of the eighteenth century came at a time when many English cathedrals were extremely decayed. They also provided architectural opportunities that he was not slow to grasp – with the general acquiescence, it must be said, of the Chapters concerned.

Wyatt's work at Lichfield, Hereford (after the fall of the West tower), Salisbury and Durham was attacked by the Society of Antiquaries and later condemned by Pugin and Ruskin as being insensitive and unnecessarily destructive. His approach was unashamedly that of the single-minded creative architect, bent on 'improving' the imperfections of buildings entrusted to him by carrying out partial reconstructions, removing monuments and screens, providing unobstructed through views from east to west ends and imposing architectural symmetry wherever he thought it desirable. At Hereford he destroyed the Norman triforium and clerestorey and rebuilt the West end in Gothic style; at Salisbury he removed the choir screen and at Durham he took inches off the face of the decayed external stonework and would, if he could, have demolished the Galilee and the Chapter House and put a spire on the crossing tower.

For all his undoubted misdeeds, Wyatt has suffered the fate of most of history's cartoon villains in being saddled with many crimes he did not actually commit. It must also be said that he was doing no more than many cultured people at the time would have thought proper. But he was only the first of several generations of energetic restorers, most of whom would have criticised his unscholarly work whilst providing good scholarly arguments for their own, not altogether dissimilar, restoration campaigns. In this though, as in many other things, France set a pace of its own by investing one man, a formidable scholar and dedicated architect–restorer, with enormous power.

Restoration: Viollet-le-Duc and the search for perfection

Eugène-Emanuel Viollet-le-Duc (1814–1879), architect and archaeologist, was an early and crucial appointment made by the French Historical Monuments Commission. Inspired by Merimée and Victor Hugo, he became France's leading mediaeval scholar, architectural theorist and (more centrally to our concerns) restorer.

There can be no doubt (the evidence is ample and visible all over France) that during the Viollet-le-Duc regime the business of the Commission went far beyond preservation intact. The recovery of an ideal and complete former state was for him a prime concern. He went so far as to say that 'to restore a building … is to re-establish it in a state of completion which may never have existed at any given moment in the past'. Even while he was working on his first major project at Vezelay in 1840, his approach, which was contrary to the sensitive policies incorporated in his briefing from the Commission, was criticised as 'the vandalism of completion'. He was, nevertheless, given his head and went on to make radical changes – in the name of architecture and history – to Sainte Chapelle, Notre Dame de Paris and Saint-Ouen in Rouen, imposing on the last an architectural homogeneity it had never possessed. During the Second Empire he controlled practically all restorations to major monuments throughout France.

Before embarking on an uncritical castigation of this programme, it needs to be put into historical context. France had been through forty years of traumatic change and destruction by the time the first General Inspector of Historical Monuments was appointed. There was a desperate need to re-establish a sense of national cultural identity. Regaining the monuments of

7.1 Conservation practice has always been coloured by the historical circumstances of the time in which it took place. Authenticity has not always been an overriding consideration. E E Viollet-le-Duc saw the role of the restorer as one of 're-establishing a state of completion which may never have existed at any given moment in the past'. Such a statement now sounds extraordinary, but the view was one quite widely held. Many of the monuments undergoing this kind of 'restoration' had, in fact, fallen into advanced disrepair. This view by Thomas Shotter Boys shows the dilapidated condition of the Sainte Chapelle, Paris (Pierre de Montreuil, 1248) with works in progress under a follower of Viollet-le-Duc in 1839. Comparison with the chapel as now seen reveals that his work went far beyond essential repair and reinstatement. The portal here seen being erected is entirely his. The roof spire had disappeared before 1839. The present one dates from 1853.

7.2a Restoration with a
vengeance: St Alban's Cathedral,
West front before restoration.
*(Reproduced by permission of
English Heritage, NMR)*

7.2b … and after restoration by
Lord Grimthorpe. *(Reproduced
by permission of English
Heritage, NMR)*

a proud past and presenting them in a way that focused attention on the artistic and architectural achievements of the nation was a natural expression of this mood.

A further note of mitigation needs to be entered in relation to Viollet-le-Duc and his British counterparts. Not only were they often averting total loss (it is easy to forget this) but, in as many cases, they were creating the very conditions – especially in relation to the townscape settings of cathedrals and chateaux – which are now seen as an admirable norm, to be preserved in 'unspoilt' completeness. We must also avoid falling into the trap of dismissing or even destroying their architectural creations simply because they do not accord with our own view of what they should have been doing. This would merely be to repeat the restorers' error of attempting to rewrite history.

The recovery of what is perceived as lost perfection may, in some circumstances, seem as desirable as the preservation of mutilated original fabric. The motives of the famous restorers were varied and a great deal more complex than they appear to be at first sight. High scholarship was regularly pressed into the service of non-scholarly ideals. Patriotism, romanticism, religious enthusiasm, advanced architectural theory and artistic ambition all contributed to the emergence of what became, in effect, a new architectural movement, greatly – but not exclusively – concerned with ancient buildings.

7.3 Durham Cathedral, the Galilee: Wyatt would, if he could, have demolished this in the name of restoration.

The reader who wishes to follow the mainstream and the many back-waters of this movement in Britain must turn to works which detail the progress of the Gothic revival, the influence of the Tractarians, the Cambridge Camden Society and the Ecclesiologists, the writings of Pugin and Ruskin and the works of the major Victorian architects. We are concerned here only with the part of the story that concerns the preservation of old buildings.

To over-generalise, nineteenth-century restoration campaigns, although based on reverence for ancient buildings, actually tended to use them as raw material in the drive for what the restorers saw as architectural perfection. The resulting visible destruction of original fabric produced its own contemporary reaction. The opponents of restoration were looking for a different kind of perfection. Whether their perfection was any more attainable is a question that lies at the heart of conservation philosophy.

Scott and Morris: 'Scrape and Anti-Scrape'

[Restoration] … means the most total destruction which a building can suffer … Do not let us deceive ourselves in this important matter; it is impossible, as impossible as to raise the dead, to restore anything that has ever been great or beautiful in architecture … The spirit of the dead workman cannot be summoned up … and as for direct and simple copying, it is palpably impossible. What copying can there be of surfaces that have been worn half an inch down? The whole finish of the work was in the half inch that has gone; if you attempt to restore that finish, you do it conjecturally; if you copy what is left … how is the new work better than the old? There was yet in the old some life, some mysterious suggestion of what it had been and of what it had lost; some sweetness in the gentle lines which rain and sun had wrought. There can be none in the brute hardness of the new …
Do not let us talk then of restoration. The thing is a lie from beginning to end.
John Ruskin, *Seven Lamps of Architecture* (The Lamp of Memory), 1849

I have before mentioned that [the beauty of the eastern parts of the Abbey] was almost wholly obliterated by the repairs effected by Sir Christopher Wren and that his work is again in a state of decay: What I would urge, then, is that it should now be restored to its original beauty. The design may generally be recovered with some degree of

certainty by fair induction from existing details of the Abbey itself, aided by old views, the model preserved in the Church, and by reference to the French cathedrals on which the design is founded.
Sir George Gilbert Scott: letter to the Sub-Dean of Westminster, March 1854

I am in this, as in other works, obliged to face right and left to combat at once two enemies from either hand, one wanting me to do too much and the other finding fault with me for doing anything at all.
Sir George Gilbert Scott on the pressures of working on St Alban's in the 1870s

Sir: My eye just now caught the word 'restoration' in the morning paper and, on looking closer, I saw that this time it is nothing less than the minster of Tewkesbury that is to be destroyed by Sir Gilbert Scott. Is it altogether too late to do something to save it – and whatever else of beautiful or historical is left to us on the sites of the ancient buildings we were once so famous for?
William Morris: letter to *Athenaeum*, 5 March 1877

The advocates of restoration have a plausible and consistent theory on which a vast amount of work of the kind has been carried out during the last half century in most of the countries of Europe. To the anti-restorationists this theory is pedantic and futile and the work which it has guided had better have been left undone …

It is no part of the present purpose to take a side in this controversy. The writer is in this matter an opportunist whose general sympathy with the opponents of restoration does not go so far as to lead him to condemn indiscriminately all undertakings of the kind. It appears indeed that no one general principle can be laid down to meet all cases …
G Baldwin Brown, *The Care of Ancient Monuments*, 1905

The Victorian restorers removed 'original' features, Perpendicular and later, and especially Georgian, and we tell them they were vandals. What they put in their stead a hundred years ago, should not that now be as sacrosanct as the Georgian pieces a hundred years old when they removed them? Should we not watch that we don't become the incorrigible vandals of a century from today?
Sir Nikolaus Pevsner: 'Scrape and Anti-Scrape' in *The Future of the Past*, 1976

'Anti-Scrape', the popular name attached to the Society for the Protection of Ancient Buildings (SPAB) when it was formed 1877, referred to the running battle between those who would protect old buildings and those who were restoring or 'scraping' them – removing plaster, cutting back the face of weathered masonry (as Wyatt did at Durham), destroying furnishings and recreating mediaeval churches (the particular object of restoration campaigns) in approved fourteenth-century 'Decorated' style, the style considered most conducive to proper Christian worship. The literary shots fired in this battle must be read in the light of what was happening at the time.

The most notable restorers were the leading church architects. Sir George Gilbert Scott (1811–1878) became the focus of the most scathing critical attacks, and with good reason. He was a tremendously prolific architect and a most expert investigator of old buildings. Although he professed to adhere to wholly commendable principles – the importance of arresting decay, of making authentic records of the found state of ancient buildings, of avoiding conjectural reinstatements – his actual performance was rarely so pure and self-denying. An exact contemporary of Viollet-le-Duc's, he brought a similar cast of mind to work on numerous national monuments, including Westminster Abbey, Ely, Hereford, Lichfield, Salisbury, Chichester, Ripon, Chester, Worcester and other cathedrals.

Although Ruskin's views, quoted above, were influential, it was not until 28 years later, when William Morris's letter appeared in the *Athenaeum* (also quoted above), that the anti-restoration forces were mobilised into a movement. Morris proposed that 'an association should be set on foot to keep a watch on old monuments (and) to protect against all "restoration" that means more than keeping out wind and weather.'

The time was ripe. There was an immediate response, as much from artists and archaeologists as from architects (some of whom were doing rather too well out of the restoration boom). The architects, however, included J F Bentley, E R Robson, J J Stevenson and, most importantly, Philip Webb (1831–1915). Webb's presence as co-founder, joined later by W R Lethaby, ensured the support of the young architects of the Arts and Crafts movement.

The formation of the new Society for the Protection of Ancient Buildings produced an interesting response from its target villain, Scott. He, it must be remembered, regarded himself as a proponent of conservative restoration, contrasting with the destructive work of (for example) Lord Grimthorpe. For the anti-scrapers the distinction was hardly worth drawing and it certainly did not deflect their fire, but Scott, nursing his bruises and counting his money, wished the Society success 'in all their reasonable endeavours'. He suggested that they should press upon the proprietors of ruined buildings the need to 'secure the tops of shattered walls from wet' and that they should have measured drawings made of 'all the unprotected architectural antiquities of our lands'. Most oddly, considering his own record, he anticipated the emerging philosophy of the Society by urging them to 'oppose… the destruction of ancient buildings, down even to those of the last century'.

Morris himself became the first Secretary of the SPAB. The Society was to have an uphill task (Grimthorpe's root-and-branch restorations at St Alban's, for example, led to an unseemly slanging match at a Royal Institute of British Architects (RIBA) meeting) but it produced at its birth a *Manifesto* which was and is a key document in the development of the philosophy of building conservation.

The SPAB Manifesto and after

It is for all these buildings, therefore, of all times and styles, that we plead, and call upon those who have to deal with them to put Protection in the place of Restoration, to stave off decay by daily care, to prop a perilous wall or mend a leaky roof by such means as are obviously meant for support or covering, and show no pretence of other art, and otherwise to resist all tampering with either the fabric or ornament of the building as it stands … Thus and only thus shall we escape the reproach of our learning being turned into a snare for us; thus, and thus only can we protect our ancient buildings and hand them down instructive and venerable to those that come after us.
William Morris: *Manifesto* of the Society for the Protection of Ancient Buildings, 1877

The reader is advised to pause at this point and read the SPAB *Manifesto* in full (Appendix 2). The *Manifesto* does not lay down specific principles or procedures as later documents do. The Society stresses today that it is not a blueprint but rather a lens through which a building and its problems are to be viewed.

It is certainly a document whose importance goes far beyond its historical context. It was the first attempt to set down basic ideals which still guide leading conservation specialists today and, if we remove from it every reference which is essentially of its own time, we are still left with a coherent and logically defensible philosophy which needs remarkably few modern glosses. When we look at later policy statements (for example, the *Venice Charter* – see Appendix 3) we shall find that the underlying thinking of the *Manifesto* has been adopted and developed rather than substantially amended. The recruiting call of a group of Victorian campaigners can still, in fact, be heard in these internationally approved conservation creeds.

There is, however, one important way in which the *Manifesto* differs from later authoritative documents like the *Charter*. In 1877 it was necessary to argue that the position being taken was a sound one and better than any of the alternatives (so, to this extent, 'right'). In most modern statements the argument is assumed to be over and the case proved. The *Venice Charter*, for example, says that: 'The conservation ... of monuments *must* have recourse to all the sciences and techniques which contribute to the ... safeguarding of the architectural heritage'; 'Restoration' [the word is used here in its dictionary sense] '*must* stop at the point where conjecture begins ... and any extra work *must* be distinct from the architectural composition and bear a contemporary stamp': 'Additions *cannot be allowed* except in so far as they do not detract' etc, etc [my emphases].

For all that *Venice* is the wise consensual view of twentieth-century conservation experts, offering a logical set of rules to guide those engaged in serious conservation work, it cannot be more than that. No such set of rules can ever represent the absolute and final truth. The bedrock principles of preservation and restoration of all kinds of art works, antiquities and monuments have continued (and will continue) to be analysed and argued over throughout the world. The fundamental questions we identified in Chapter 2 – the what and the why and the how – have engaged philosophers, art historians and conservators up to the present time.

We have already set out, in Chapters 4 and 5, a number of kinds of buildings, great and small, which, through the ages, have presented themselves for preservation as monuments. This attempt at definition has largely been a matter of reportage rather than argument. As a matter of observable historical fact, the desire to preserve such buildings has preceded, and has never been deflected by, subsequent theorising. But what follows from that desire – the means of preservation; the choice of one course of action in preference to another – has been deeply influenced by the thoughts and writings of theorists and expert practitioners and, as we have already noted, they have spoken with different voices at different times.

In this connection we have briefly noted important players like James Wyatt (1746–1813), Karl Friedrich Schinkel (1781–1841), George Gilbert Scott (1811–1878), Viollet-le-Duc (1814–1879), John Ruskin (1819–1900) and William Morris (1834–1896). We should note now the work of Alois Riegl (1857–1905) Max Dvorak (1874–1921) and Cesare Brandi (1906–1988), all of whom have had considerable influence on conservation philosophy and practice throughout Europe.

Riegl, an art historian, was from 1902 the General Conservator in the Austrian Central Commission for Antiquities. In his short active life he was a prolific and original writer (one of his early works linked the history of Oriental art with that of the West). In 1903 he published *The Modern Cult of Monuments*, a major historical and philosophical study which, interestingly, distinguished between those buildings created as 'intended' monuments and those which became perceived as monuments by later ages, a phenomenon commented on in Chapter 4 above. His follower, Dvorak, was a powerful opponent of unnecessary destruction in the name of restoration and a pioneer in the conservation of townscape and the natural environment.

With Brandi we come close to our own time. He was a man of many parts: a poet, art critic, professor of art history and conservator. He was, from 1939, first Director of the Central Institute of Restoration in Rome and became an important contributor to the conservation work of UNESCO. Italy's enormous artistic wealth has made it a testing ground – arguably a battle ground – *par excellence* for a diversity of views on the theory and practice of restoration of art works and monuments. Brandi's published works have been amongst the most influential in their field. It may be said that the SPAB *Manifesto* marked out the ground for the *Venice Charter* and its successors, but the design of the superstructure owes a great deal to Brandi.

The extent to which theoretical ideals can be translated into useful codes of practice may be judged by the reader from the examples given in the Appendices. My own view is that we are getting better at it and will get better still if we look critically at the record of past attempts. The somewhat peremptory bylaw tone of the 1964 *Venice Charter* ('must stop' – 'cannot be allowed') makes a striking contrast with the appeal to recent painful experience in the 1877 *Manifesto*. The *Charter* (like its predecessor, the *Athens Charter* of 1931 and its successors, the *Recommendations of the UNESCO Paris Conferences* of 1968 and 1972) was an important milestone but practitioners working on fully employed 'high street' historic buildings will not, perhaps, turn to it regularly for guidance. The *Burra Charter* of 1981, by contrast, has a rather more practical flavour, insisting that detailed knowledge of the building or place is the key to correct action, a recipe that is clearly as applicable to the humble cottage as to the magnificent palace.

*The conservation policy appropriate to a place must first be
determined by an understanding of its cultural significance and its
physical condition.*
Australia ICOMOS *Burra Charter*

This brings us back to what was said at the very beginning. There are no absolutely infallible commandments except, perhaps, this one: 'Know your building'. In this, the establishment of 'cultural significance' as defined in Burra should precede all other considerations.

The test for both the practitioner and his or her guiding philosophy is what actually happens when a particular problem has to be tackled. Some clearly preferable solutions may be completely blocked off for practical or legal reasons, whilst the remaining alternatives may offer differing combinations of advantage and disadvantage. With a building in everyday commercial, industrial or domestic use, which is not a great rarity or a considerable work of architecture but which is nevertheless deserving of care and respect, the practitioner may find that the dog-eared and, at first sight, rather inflexible SPAB statement provides a surprisingly helpful starting point and the *Burra Charter* (Appendix 4) an excellent working companion.

In the next chapters we shall look at some recurring problems and examine the philosophical arguments for and against different approaches and see how far, if at all, we need to bring different values to bear in different circumstances.

CHAPTER 8

The Practice of Preservation: Philosophy in Action

No single yardstick

As soon as we embark on the business of marking out particular buildings for special care we are confronted by the questions 'How special?' 'What kinds of care?' It soon becomes apparent that different buildings call for different kinds of care, permitting or prohibiting different kinds of intervention. There is no single yardstick.

A Saxon church and a 1930s super-cinema are at opposite ends of the spectrum in terms of antiquity, artistic ambition and structural character. In one case, the archaeological evidence contained in every original stone and every tool mark is of such importance that the slightest, most thoughtless interference may be the cause of irreparable loss. At the same time, the succession of alterations and additions that have been made in the building's thousand or more years of existence seem to us to be precious biographical records. Such a powerful relic of the past demands that we approach it with reverence as well as technical skill, leaving it, so far as possible, to tell its own story.

The super-cinema, by contrast, is a symbol of its time in a rather different way. Its principal interest lies in its original architectural design and decoration, which speak to us – and may to later ages – of the society and the view of leisure that produced it. Structurally and technically, it has some interest which may loosely be termed archaeological, but most of the materials and techniques employed in its construction are still commonly used. Later alterations to convert it to (say) a carpet warehouse are likely to be viewed by most people as subtracting from rather than adding to its significance. Such a building attracts admiration or enthusiasm rather than reverence. Most people would think it important to keep it architecturally intact, if it is to tell a story worth telling.

To say that the one 'demands that we approach it' in a certain way, whilst in the other case 'most people would think' that it should be treated in a rather different way, is to emphasise that a kind of sensitivity, rather than obedience to a set of immutable rules, is at work. In both cases, however, it is reasonable to lay importance on the story that the building has to tell. If we re-examine the variety of non-utilitarian motives for preserving buildings, we will find that at the heart of all of them is the feeling that old buildings are conveying valued messages from the past. The business of the preserver of buildings must be to see that those messages reach us and are transmitted to our successors without becoming garbled. In this sense it makes no difference whether we are working on a Saxon church or a super-cinema. Both need special care for the same fundamental reason. They do not, however, call for the same detailed procedures and techniques.

The fact that different cases may need to be approached in different ways can lead on to the thought that it is all a matter of the relative importance of the buildings in question. The simplest solution (so the argument might go on) would seem to be to grade the buildings from the most to the least important and give them exactly correlated degrees of care.

There is just enough validity in this idea to make it dangerous. In Britain our lists of historic buildings do, in fact, attempt some kind of relative valuation which, at least at the upper (Grade I) end, looks reasonable, but the quotation from John Fidler at the head of Chapter 6 contains a warning. Fidler makes the important point that the external circumstances of the building – the immediacy of a threat to its survival – must necessarily change our perception of its importance. He might have added that this changed perception often prompts investigations which throw up new knowledge and necessitate re-evaluation. Also, more fundamentally, a grading system inevitably leads to unlike buildings with unlike qualities and unlike problems being straitjacketed into a single hierarchy. We cannot judge what degree of care needs to be exercised in a particular case today by referring to some past attempt at quality grading.

In organising our own thoughts, however, some broad 'sorting' of the population of buildings can be both justifiable and helpful. To take only one example, it is, as we have already suggested, reasonable to distinguish between buildings that are in – and benefit from being in – modern use and those which are clearly quite incapable of any use. Again, a building that is the product of extinct craft practices is in a different league from one whose care calls only for materials and techniques readily available today. Distinctions of this kind will be made from time to time throughout the rest of this study. The question of the relative 'importance' of the building measured against some absolute scale of values will not arise.

Conservation and compromise

Starting from a completely uncompromising position (as it were, off the left hand edge of the SPAB *Manifesto*), is there not a case for according our precious buildings the same kind of care as museum objects? Should we not strive to preserve every last atom of the original fabric in the state in which it has come down to us, making all work of necessary conservation wholly reversible, recognising that future generations may have access to better techniques?

An instructive comparison (since it involves both museum technology and building fabric) can, perhaps, be made with the conservation of damaged frescos. One (Florentine) approach – and it would be wrong to give the impression that there is total unanimity in the museum conservation world – is to strip the painting from the wall together with the top layer of plaster which has become an inseparable part of it; deal with the causes of chemical attack within the plaster and paint; mount the stripped layers (using reversible techniques) on to an inert backing, piecing every tiny fragment of the original artist's work into its correct position, even from areas otherwise devastated by damp and salts; then to complete, by painting anew, the missing or irreparably damaged parts of the composition where their character is known, in a manner close to the original but clearly distinguishable from it (for example, by the introduction of striations over the new work). The final step is to remount the completed work in or near to its original position, but isolated from the risks which caused the original damage.

The ideal that this procedure represents is not altogether irrelevant in a building conservation context – but note that it illustrates how even museum conservators have to compromise at times. A wall painting is not, in fact, a self-sufficient work of art to be treated in isolation, like an easel painting or a drawing in a sketch book. It was made on, and the paint was combined permanently with, the fresh plaster (hence 'fresco') in the process of creating a decorated room. The conservator's new inert backing has nothing whatever to do with the conditions under which the painting was originally produced. If the conserved work is seen finally to be some-thing separate from the building structure, then we must admit that the artist's intention has been modified and to that extent the whole meticu-lously careful process has led to loss in terms of both historical record and aesthetic intent. If, on the other hand, steps are taken to conceal the back-ing and to pretend that nothing much has happened, is that not precisely the kind of falsification that the conservator has been at pains to avoid in the newly painted passages?

The problems arise from the fact that conservation in these terms is a highly artificial procedure which, for the best of reasons, attempts to arrest, if not to eliminate, natural processes of change and decay. It goes far beyond simple maintenance (which, in the case of a wall painting, might mean the occasional touch of a feather duster and some prudent steps to control atmospheric conditions) moving into a realm where philosophical argument is bound to arise. The conservator may say:

> *Of course we have had to compromise a little, but the painting is now as safe as we can make it. Nothing has been done that cannot be undone if our judgment is later thought to have been wrong. We have made some of our work almost unnoticeable for aesthetic reasons but, even so, it is not completely invisible and experts will see at a glance what has been done. For lovers of art who are not interested in the business of conservation, the conservation processes have not interfered unduly with their enjoyment. The artist's creation is as complete as it now can be. It would not be here to be enjoyed if we had left it alone.*

These arguments sound almost unanswerable, but there will still be those who will say that the interference with the original material has nev-ertheless been too drastic and in some respects is irreversible. They will point out that many present-day conservers attempt to avoid stripping altogether. The impression of completeness (they will say) is quite false and the devices used to distinguish modern from original work simply laugh-able. There may also be a division between those whose reverence for the original material is such that they would wish the surviving painted frag-ments to be surrounded by unpainted areas, and those whose concern is so much centred on artistic appreciation that they would insist on the con-servator's infill being completely invisible to anyone except an expert.

A painting – even a fresco – is a simple artefact compared to a building made of masonry, timber, plaster, fired clay, iron and glass, with foundations in the earth, exterior exposed to the elements and interior subjected to continual wear in use. Some buildings do, in some respects (including the demands they make on the practitioner), have the character of museum objects, but the problems they pose are likely to be far more complex and the compromises they lead to at least as open to debate as any that face the museum conservator.

Ruins

... The eie and mind is no less affected with these stately ruines than they would have been when standing and entire. They breed in generous minds a kind of pittie; and set the thoughts a-worke ...
John Aubrey, antiquary (1626–1697)

Even the most down-to-earth person can feel his imagination stirred by a ruin ... At Carcassonne in France during a bitterly cold February day the wind banging the shutters of Viollet-le-Duc's restoration created an uncanny sensation. This was the sort of feeling that the eighteenth century visitor tried to induce in himself from a ruin.
M W Thompson Ruins: *Their Preservation and Display*, 1981

However much solicitude may be lavished on a ruin, it has no indefinite life ... It is quite likely that the removal of the protective layer of fallen debris at the base of a ruin hastens the erosion of dressed stone and thereby shortens the life of what must in any case have a finite life. Here we are making use of the ruin by rendering it intelligible to the visitor, both for pleasure and instruction ...
Thompson, ibid.

The eighteenth-century landscaping at Fountains and Rievaulx is entirely misleading as to the real appearance of those abbeys in mediaeval times and certainly gives the visitor the wrong impression of their original aspect, but it would be unthinkable to alter it; the landscaping has assumed the importance of a monument in its own right.
Thompson, ibid.

Most ancient monuments have spent at least half their lives, if not more, as ruins and not as buildings in use. It is just as relevant to study, record and understand the ruined phase of their history as it is the other.

Gill Chitty, 'A Prospect of Ruins', *Transactions of the Association for Studies in the Conservation of Historic Buildings*, 1987

Conflicts over what constitutes the right treatment are least taxing when the building is simply a venerated object of no conceivable practical use – a sort of outsized exhibit. The preservation of the remains of, say, Fountains Abbey presents special problems – but they could hardly be as daunting as those facing a building like the Great Palm House at Kew, whose proper appreciation depends as much on its designed use as on its architectural character and whose deterioration is accelerated by that use.

The preservation of Fountains must take account of the fact that, as well as being the remnant of an imposing work of architecture and a document of the shock of the Dissolution, it has become an evocative object in a designed landscape. The motive for preservation is, in fact, many-layered, but the only generally recurring philosophical puzzle with such a monument is how to preserve its integrity without denying its nature. The natural destiny of a ruin is, after all, that it becomes steadily covered with ivy or old man's beard and that pieces of masonry drop off from time to time. On the whole we like our ruins to look ancient and crumbly, our churchyard monuments to be mossy and overgrown – but, at the same time, we want to arrest the processes of dissolution at a point we find pleasing.

Although at first sight the care of ruins may be regarded as an exceptionally pure form of conservation, using techniques as scientific and single-minded as those of the museum conservator, the technology is, in fact, very often being pressed into the service of art. The finished effect does not represent a 'natural' state of the monument, neither can it be said to have achieved the perfectly sustained, nearly unchanging state of a museum object. It is in many ways a work created to fulfil instructional, aesthetic and emotional needs.

Stabilising ruined walls, protecting their tops and removing damaging growth all contribute to what is, in fact, an artificial state of affairs – albeit one which can be held in place without declaring the fact too loudly. We are so used to seeing these things done that they no longer seem to be compromises, but that is what they are. Our curiosity about the great abbeys and what became of them can, by this discreet intervention, be stimulated. Our aesthetic instincts ('Look – this is a view that has inspired great painters, and how little it has changed!') can also be satisfied. The precise methods adopted may be open to argument but, if we are going to preserve these things at all, we are going to adopt some such time-denying compromises. And since there are no questions of utility to take into account, the degree of intervention can be limited to the minimum needed to produce the desired effect.

That minimum will invariably include the measures adopted to present the monument in an intelligible manner. This raises another question. Should we ever attempt re-erection, making use of original material found on the site (anastylosis) in order to assist public understanding of what has been preserved? We will look at this in Chapter 11, when we come to consider other forms of reconstruction.

Having looked at this one special aspect of conservation we have already tripped over a paradox, in that the conservator of ruins is required to do a great deal while appearing to do nothing (see Chitty, *loc cit* and her quoted authorities for a detailed consideration of this question).

Before leaving this subject, it will be noted, from the first quotation from Thompson, above, that whilst we now deal with ruins in scientific, scholarly ways, deep emotional responses are as alive today as they were in Aubrey's time.

But ruins are relatively uncomplicated objects. We should now, perhaps, attempt to propose a common-sense approach to conservation which leaves to one side the archaeologically exacting demands of what I have called the 'outsize exhibit', not because they are irrelevant – the fundamental issues are always the same – but because such a structure arguably raises fewer and less perplexing questions than a building in use.

Pause for philosophical reflection

The idea that there can be alternative philosophical approaches to the preservation of buildings is seriously misleading. Correctness cannot be watered down. You should either do a job properly or not do it at all.
Purist

A sound philosophy is one which points in the right general direction – that of truthfulness. Its precise application must depend on the building and its circumstances. If I am in command of all the facts, then the building itself will tell me what to do.
Pragmatist

Preservation is a completely artificial procedure, interfering with
natural processes of decay and obsolescence. Preservation philosophies
are therefore necessarily artificial. They are generally used to justify
an approach already decided upon.
Cynic

Consider the above three viewpoints before proceeding further. You may feel that the arguments presented so far have led you to see that there is some gleam of truth in all three positions. If, however, it is accepted that building conservation is not a precise science but an art, the first must be seen as too rigid. As Powys puts it: 'It is wise not to lay down dogmatic rules, for when they are made one is apt to be confronted by a case where they do not work.' The fact that modern practitioners have access to an armoury of technologies does not make the 'correct' course of action susceptible to precise calculation.

For all that it, too, contains a sharp observation, the third statement goes too far in the opposite direction, concerning itself only with utility and dismissing all other preservation efforts as 'artificial'. It takes no account of the fact that human beings have spiritual as well as physical needs. It should by now need no arguing that a very large number of people – not only those with a scholarly interest – wish to see old buildings preserved. Many of them would probably find it difficult to analyse their feelings on the subject; others might offer reasons ranging from the purely aesthetic to the frankly defensive – the need for tangible 'roots'. The fact that such demands are not always well articulated and the public benefits cannot be measured in terms of rentals and percentages, does not invalidate the demands or make the benefits unreal. It is the conservator's none-too-easy task to sustain enjoyment without creating a situation so artificial that it amounts to falsehood.

The second statement might be criticised on the grounds that it is too pragmatic to be safe. It is all very well to recognise that no two cases are quite alike and that a building must be allowed to speak with its own true voice – but surely we need firmer direction than this?

It is the central argument of this study that it is not the imposition of some ready-made philosophical system but a full understanding of the problem that is most likely to produce a defensible solution. The idea that knowledge of the building is paramount and that all judgments must be based on that knowledge is surely not to be questioned. This view also offers practical advantages, in guiding one away from the thrall of a too-rigid set of commandments. Knowing a building intimately hones sensibilities to the particular task in hand, identifies necessary constraints and sets down the rules for that particular building. Whether, thereafter, and having regard to all the other circumstances affecting the life of the building, the solutions adopted produce a satisfactory result will depend, as it always must, on the personal skill of the practitioner.

There is a logic about this kind of approach which enables practitioners (this applies as much to those who exercise statutory controls as to those initiating works) to question what they are doing and frame defensible solutions even when facing situations outside their previous experience.

The nature and interest of a building

The primary purpose of repair is to restrain the process of decay without damaging the character of buildings or monuments, altering the features which give them historic or architectural importance or unnecessarily disturbing or destroying historic fabric.
English Heritage Advisory Leaflet, *Principles of Repair*

It is obviously necessary to define the precise nature of the special interest one is seeking to protect. What kind of building are we dealing with and what are the non-utilitarian motives (very likely more than one) behind the desire to preserve? Refer to Chapters 4 and 5, but do not be too bewitched by the section headings, which are designed to be memorable rather than definitive. Can the building be described as a work of art in its own right? An example of vernacular traditions and crafts? Was it the home of a famous person? – and so on. Physical and documentary investigation is an essential part of this process and one must always be ready to correct or restate received notions.

The structural nature (in this connection not to be confused with condition), the plan form and the manner of use of the building, can all be important components of historic interest. Clearly, an intervention which damages our – or a future generation's – understanding of the building negates the whole purpose of the exercise. To take an obvious example, an old house whose interest derives in significant measure from internal modifications made for the specialised requirements of a famous artist, would be devastated by the elimination of studio and gallery to provide a more convenient plan for modern use – and the offence is compounded if boast is then made of having 'restored' the house to its original form.

A large part of the art of the conserver of buildings in use is that of achieving utility without loss of interest. In some circumstances past damage can be made good and the interest of the building even enhanced without falling into the twin traps of conjectural restoration or 'improving on' (or destroying inconvenient aspects of) history.

Investigation before action

A thorough understanding of the historic development of a building … is a necessary preliminary to its repair.

In addition to [this] analysis the detailed design of repairs should also be preceded by a survey of … structural defects and an investigation of the nature and condition of … materials and … the causes and processes of decay.
English Heritage Advisory Leaflet, *Principles of Repair*

A detailed investigation of the building, accompanied by whatever documentary research may also be possible, is the first step to be taken in any conservation project. This, again, is not simply a practical necessity, directed solely to the physical condition of the building. If, as has been suggested, an historic building is a body of evidence, conveying messages from the past (this is how we built; this was the architectural taste of our time; this is how we wished to be remembered; this is how we planned our houses, streets, towns; this is how we lived, worked, played, governed and worshipped; this reflects the taste of a famous person, the condition of a wealthy merchant or an artisan, and so on), then we must know the building and its historical context intimately. In no other way can we avoid the risk of eroding the evidential value and aesthetic integrity of the building.

This investigation should establish the facts about the character, interest and present state of the building. The physical condition of the structure, its inherent strengths and weaknesses, the effects of past alterations and evidence of acquired defects (fungal and insect attacks, overloading problems, structural movements and so on) are all matters in which building professionals, at least, may feel fairly secure in their judgements. Even so, there is a risk of misdiagnosis and loss of historically interesting fabric if the practitioner is not familiar with historical building practices.

Failing to observe conditions which are common to most buildings of a particular kind and date (for example, peculiarities of floor framing or the lack of bond between face and backing brickwork in an eighteenth-century terrace house) or, no less seriously, identifying them as defects, can lead to fatally wrong decisions. Cracks, distortions, sags and bulges that occurred early in the life of a building often represent non-life-threatening adjustments whose existence should be anticipated but not feared. Stabilisation may occasionally be called for, but the attempt to 'correct' all movement and iron out every unevenness can trigger more problems than it solves – as well as eroding the interest and authenticity of the fabric.

Many perfectly healthy buildings have been wrecked by destructive 'cures' prescribed for their supposed defects or by being pressed into uses for which they were inherently unsuitable.

The ill-informed rarely damage historic buildings for the sake of economy – if anything, the reverse is the case. For example, office conversions of Georgian terraced houses commonly suffer from overkill. Numerous cases have occurred of good, original ironmongery in architecturally modest houses (front door knockers, shutter furniture and so on) being replaced by completely inappropriate brass fittings because 'our tenants will expect everything to be in period'. There is actually no contradiction – from a developer's point of view – in this statement. The tenants are probably looking for a certain kind of 'prestige' accommodation in which part of the cachet derives from the fact that the building has some sort of pedigree (perhaps more than the occupying firm can claim!). Provided it looks suitably elegant, then what can be said about its past history is probably more important than what it is. If the fact that the original builders used iron is thought about at all (and it almost certainly won't be) it will be seen as an unfortunate lapse which has now been splendidly made good. We will find similar motives at work when we come to consider the use of substitute materials (see page 101).

The arguments advanced for this kind of varnishing of history are not completely unanswerable, even in hard commercial terms. Some occupiers do, in fact, take pride in careful preservation, even accepting operational inconvenience for the sake of a building whose original qualities they value. From the point of view of the building conservator, certainly, there can be no philosophical defence for using an old building as raw material for the creation of a falsehood, however saleable the finished product may be. To destroy original material unnecessarily cannot be what we mean by preservation – and to attempt to improve on the past is simply to garble the story that the building has been preserved to relate.

The story, of course, is never complete. A building can never completely escape its own time, whatever misfortunes may befall it, but neither can it remain locked changeless in that time. There is an awesomeness, which most of us have experienced, even if rarely, about a building which has survived almost untouched (or has been cunningly reinstated so that it feels untouched) – a place where not only the visible masonry, wood, metal, plaster, decorations, furnishings and floor coverings are all appropriate to the date of original occupation, but one where the daylight and night lighting, mode of heating, air temperature, draughts and smells (cooking, laundry, floor polish, damp clothing in the hall) all speak of that time. The strangeness of entering a house formerly occupied by an elderly person, still retaining gas or oil light, distempered walls, linoleum, cane sink, brick copper and yet a feeling of daily use in this form, is sharpened by one's awareness that this kind of special perfection is extremely fragile.

Even the most completely preserved buildings have to be viewed through the circumstances that our own time has placed them in. When the elderly householder referred to above dies, the next occupants may cherish the building, rejecting double glazing, wall-to-wall carpets and even central heating as thoroughly inappropriate, but the installation of what they see as bare essentials – probably roof insulation, electric light and power and modern cooking and bathing facilities – will affect the character of the building and change quite radically the experience of being in it.

Except where the building is to be frozen in its present state as an exhibit (like the National Trust for Scotland's Glasgow Tenement House – an example not far removed from the hypothetical case set out above) we have to accept that continued use forces compromises of a different order from those required of the museum conservator. It should not be necessary to point out that the more unsympathetic the occupation – the more drastically the present use departs from the originally intended use – the more difficult it is to avoid harming an historic building. 'Harm' in this context, it will be realised, refers to understanding and enjoyment as well as to the physical state of the fabric. Our initial investigation of the building should, therefore, include consideration of its sensitivity in different circumstances of use.

Compromises can rarely be avoided completely, but they must be based on a complete understanding of what is at stake in each particular case. A manner of use which totally obscures the building's interest is not much more acceptable than one which dangerously overloads its floors.

Degrees of intervention

Most practitioners will not be dealing with unemployable museum pieces but fully occupied 'high street' listed buildings that have to earn a living in the modern world. They will face very different practical problems from those confronting the guardian of an unoccupied palace, a mediaeval ruin or an 'as found' exhibition house. Nevertheless, their safest starting point in looking at any conservation problem is the assumption that the building will be best served by limiting physical intervention to the practical minimum. How far one is able to go in achieving this ideal will depend partly on the circumstances of the building, but in any case it is always wise (to adapt some of Morris's words) to stave off decay by daily care and put protection before (if not always to the exclusion of) restoration.

> *The authenticity of a historic building ... depends crucially on its design and on the integrity of its fabric. The unnecessary replacement of historic fabric, no matter how carefully the work is carried out, will have an adverse effect ... and seriously reduce its value as a source of historical information.*
> English Heritage Advisory Leaflet, *Principles of Repair*

Reasons of practical necessity will always be produced (and must sometimes be accepted) for carrying out radical works to an old building, but good practical reasons can also be advanced for urging minimum disturbance. The practical and the philosophical arguments are not, in fact, mutually exclusive, but tightly entwined.

From both viewpoints, the unnecessary disturbance of sound and stable conditions should always be avoided. This may be obvious when we are dealing with the delicately poised equilibrium of a fragile structure of great age. It is just as relevant when we are considering something as simple as, say, the repointing of plain, relatively modern brickwork. If the work is not closely supervised, bad raking out or wrong mortar mixes may trigger off previously non-existent problems and actually threaten the building whose life we are trying to extend. In this connection the unsightliness of bad work should always be taken as a warning that other, less visible, kinds of damage may have been done.

A question to be asked before embarking on practically any works to an historic building is: 'Is it actually necessary – for the life and health of the building – to do this?'

The pressure of circumstances

Whatever the answer to this last question may be, there will frequently be pressure to do more or to preserve less. The pressure commonly arises from the desire of owners to push property utilisation to its limits so as to obtain maximum return in terms of performance and profits. This state of affairs is often made less negotiable by the fact that many owners, investors or developers initiating major works are, in fact, reliant on funding from agencies having no interest whatever in the building as such. *Their* sole concern is with financial security and with return on investment, but they can effectively dictate terms to their borrowers who will, in turn, incorporate them into their instructions to their own professional advisers.

Anyone involved at any level in the care or control of historic buildings will know that destructive schemes, in which total replacement of perfectly sound floors and other major structural elements is presented as utterly unavoidable, are of regular occurrence. If those who are financing the project insist on levels of structural performance, floor loading, fire-resistance, sound and thermal insulation and rental levels exactly comparable with those of a modern construction, the scene is set for large-scale destruction. The building may be particularly pleasant to live or work in, especially attractive to a certain kind of user and able to command a respectable rent; it may have a very long record of satisfactory use, exhibit no unusual structural problems and impose nothing unreasonable in the way of restraints on occupation – but if its materials and construction are not amenable to calculation and certification, then from the point of view of some financial backers it will be regarded as having failed all tests.

The best of engineers cannot, in all conscience, present convincing proof that an elderly (and, in present-day terms, unconventionally framed) wood floor will sustain even the loads that it has been clearly carrying all its life. It may be obvious that the original timber is much superior to available modern timber but it is difficult to say how superior – and it is in any case undeniable that generations of gas plumbers and electricians will have chiselled away at the members. An informed judgment is not what the client is seeking. The only way to fulfil the brief is to design a new structure.

Responsible conservation specialists are not excused of all duty to the building and to future generations in these circumstances, and they should certainly not tailor their advice to what they think their clients will find acceptable. Their recommendations should be firm and persuasive – but they may yet find themselves faced with having to turn down a commission rather than do what they know to be wrong. And, incidentally, the fact that there is someone else ready and willing to do the job should not encourage them to damage their own reputations.

In this kind of situation (and recognising that a great deal of the work carried out on historic buildings is – and will continue to be – in inexpert and even unsympathetic hands) the officials exercising statutory controls have a vital role to play. It is a demanding task, since controllers have to deal with what they see before them. They cannot reject a scheme on the grounds that it is only worth half marks and that a more intelligent applicant with a better choice of advisers might eventually come forward with a thoroughly commendable scheme. The initiatives are all in the hands of others, leaving the official in the unsatisfactory position of attempting to steer the vehicle from the back seat.

It is a relatively simple matter (and the legal powers are best designed for this purpose) to forbid clearly harmful works. It is not so easy to promote desirable works or to turn a ham-fisted but well-intentioned scheme into a good one – unless, of course, one enjoys the added advantage of being able to authorise or withhold financial help. In many cases the official will have to engage in delicate negotiation and, unless he or she has the necessary technical know-how, judgments may be faulty. Acceptance of an applicant's radical proposals without question can amount to dereliction of duty. A building may be perfectly capable of full beneficial use (perhaps not the intensity of use desired by the applicant) without destructive works. It is necessary for the controller to be in command of all the facts and, in particular, to have access to whatever specialised knowledge is required to counter, if the need arises, the technical forces marshalled on the other side.

CHAPTER 9

The Practice of Preservation: Grounds for Argument

We are now in the thick of the argument. From here on it would be unwise to read into the paragraph headings anything more than a broad indication of content. Every subject tackled raises side issues, forbidding any kind of tidy progression from one isolated topic to another.

Degrees of violence

In the last chapter we highlighted – and now need to examine further – a fundamental conflict, crudely represented as 'developer versus preserver', which must be present to some degree in any project where commercial gain forms part of the equation. In the experience of many readers this is likely to mean most projects. Two nearly opposed philosophies are at work: one viewing the building as an inheritance to be safeguarded, the other seeing it as an opportunity to be exploited.

The resolution of this conflict, so that the two forces end up pulling in more or less the same direction, requires professional skill of a high order. Where skill is lacking, exploitation will reign supreme. The question will no longer be what kinds of intervention can be justified but what degree of violence the building can stand. In these circumstances the statutory controls may be tested to the limit, since some developers will push as far as they can toward total destruction and renewal, making only those concessions they deem to be necessary to avoid over-lengthy confrontations carrying the risk of defeat and financial loss.

9.1 This *Punch* cartoon, mocking the idea of the 'preserved amenity', gasping for life as an isolated blob of prettiness, appeared in 1951. At that time there was not a single inch of motorway, let alone a motorway flyover, in the country. As a prediction of things to come in the following decades, however, it turned out to be no joke.

The philosophical implications of such collisions are, however, not of interest to statutory controllers alone. We have already observed that much may be learned by studying extreme cases.

Consider, for example, the building 'preserved' as a façade and nothing else. Pressure for this kind of radical treatment of old buildings is found wherever extremely high land values coincide with demand for a particular type of accommodation normally associated with new buildings. Rightly or wrongly, façade preservation has been permitted so often in such cases that some architects, engineers and contractors specialise in it. Interestingly, genuine conservation experts are almost unanimous in condemning the practice, whilst the façade-proppers invariably claim to be doing it out of a public-spirited concern for architectural conservation – because, in fact, 'it's what the conservationists want'.

Do they? Should they ever? The reader will, by now, be getting used to the idea that there is not going to be a simple answer – but that is not to say that such matters are to be discussed only in terms of personal whim, current fashion or short-term expediency. If building preservation is to have any kind of sensible basis there must be a process of logical reasoning to go through. Effective advocacy demands it.

We are at once up against an acute difficulty, even when we are talking to our allies. Our general education system leaves most people ignorant of – certainly lacking a vocabulary to discuss – the one science and the one art which touches nearly every minute of their lives. Despite the manifest popularity of building preservation, there is relatively little knowledge of the nature of buildings or the history of architecture in the population at large. Instincts may be sound enough, but an ability to argue at any other level is often lacking. Many a preservation battle begins with a confrontation between those who know that part of their heritage is under attack but cannot effectively defend it and those who have no real understanding of what the fuss is about but are well able to look after their own interests.

The duty of the conservation specialist, to preserve the past and make it intelligible for present and future generations, and the duty of the specialist in office to represent a 'force of intelligent belief in the mind of the people' (see the quotation from Baldwin Brown on page 26) are vitally important. No less important for the official is the ability to face opposition with reasoned argument.

The opposed mindset that one is most often faced with, tends to look at historic buildings with a collector's eye (antiques and bygones are easier to understand than buildings), seeing them as an assemblage of more or less portable period mementoes attached to an otherwise neutral display

9.2 The Chapel House, Bexleyheath. A tiny house in the form of a chapel, originally an 'eye-catcher' in a designed landscape by Capability Brown, left stranded alongside a busy traffic roundabout.

frame. To those who think like this, the interesting 'features' must actually benefit from a setting of crisp cement pointing, smooth wall plaster and level floors and ceilings. Their standard openings include: 'Tell us which are the historic bits and we'll see that they are beautifully preserved' – or, without the gift-wrapping, 'How much of this is listed, then?'

Skin-deep preservation

The controller must dispose of the memento idea before it even begins to take root. The ideas to be marshalled are fundamental to any reasoned view of conservation. They are particularly relevant to the argument about façade – or any form of 'skin-deep' – preservation.

1. A building is a building, not an accidental collection of elements of varying degrees of value and attractiveness. Its form and its plan have been determined by practical necessity and architectural skill, its construction by the building traditions, craft practices and common materials of its time and place, and its ornamental and artistic aspects by the nature of its occupancy and the taste of the period. All these aspects have documentary importance and they are closely intertwined.

9.3a Hereford.
Preservation after
a fashion: a sawn-off
timber-framed fragment
propped up as an
irrelevant ornament
attached to a modern
development.

9.3b Edinburgh.
Preservation after
another fashion: an
antique masonry façade
stuck to a modern
building.

2. All buildings, architect designed or vernacular, can be observed to have an inbuilt grammar and syntax which cannot be substantially interfered with without damaging the interest or (at worst) producing a sort of historical gibberish. It is easy to demonstrate that this is so with fully literate classical architecture, which has clear parallels to the structure of language, but it is just as true for, say, a timber-framed building and, at a less sophisticated level, an artisan's cottage.

3. Statutory protection in Britain recognises that this is so. Buildings are hardly ever listed in part. List descriptions do not define the extent of protection; they simply identify the building – which is protected as a whole, inside and out, structure and ornament.

If we accept these guidelines (and I hope you will agree that 1 and 2 contain some fairly self-evident truths, whilst 3 is plainly factual), we should be able to construct some sensible criticisms of façade preservation.

It is at least questionable whether a façade should ever be treated as a piece of decorative wrapping to be peeled off and applied to any new building desired on the site. A façade raises expectations about the building whose public face it presents. A grand stuccoed Regency façade may make some effort to look like a north Italian palace and that may be the first of many qualities attracting our admiration, but if it has front doors at regular intervals, if the spacing of the windows, the divisions between the first floor balconies and the placing of the chimney stacks reflect a rhythm of separate occupancies between party walls, then we are perfectly aware that it is not a palace. Knowing that we are looking, in fact, at a terrace of houses once occupied by people of some social ambition for whom it seemed appropriate to live behind a palatial façade, in no way reduces its interest. In some ways the ambiguity enhances our pleasure, since we read in it an interesting chapter of our national history.

Examine this case further. Without actually searching for explicit signals, we are aware that the windows of the 'palace' look out from dining rooms, drawing rooms and bedchambers, rather than rooms of state occasion. The little dormer windows in the garret light what were once the meaner rooms of the servants. We are fairly confident – because we know how such buildings were lived in – that each front door opens on to an entrance hall and a staircase and we have some expectations about the general plan arrangements, the nature of the internal plaster ornament and the marble chimney pieces. At the back we suppose that each house will have a plain brick elevation overlooking a long and narrow walled garden. The fact that the houses may by now have been divided into flats or converted to offices, that some of the chimney pieces have probably been torn out, that gaslight has been replaced by electricity, and coal fires by central heating will also be in our minds, but we may still nurture some hope that our own time has not dealt too violently with what we feel we know about the place.

Grossly misused, such a façade might find itself attached to a modern block with undivided floor areas. The illusion of domestic occupation, with room lights of differing intensity coming on at different times of the evening in an unpredictable pattern, at once gives way to the mechanical appearance of uniform office lighting behind every window. The windows themselves reveal a single space of limitless depth and width, making non-sense of the party divisions implied in the façade. With only one or two of the original front doors in use, the others will probably have been converted to windows, at once destroying an important part of the historic interest of the terrace. Alternatively, all the entrance bridges over the front basement areas may have been left in place but with front doors disused and sealed. Their dusty, unswept steps announce unmistakably what has happened. Entering the building from the front (the rear probably looks like any other office block) all expectations raised by the façade will immediately be dashed. It is revealed as being nothing more than a face transplant.

Add to all these mishaps an additional storey replacing the low garret (it is usually done by stretching the façade up to form a classical attic above the main cornice, the rationalisation being that, correctly designed, it will then look even more like an Italian palazzo) and, above that, two storeys of over-sized dormers set in an uncharacteristic mansard. The net result: something like nine-tenths of the fabric of the 'preserved' building has been lost and most of its original character destroyed. Such a building is no more than a souvenir of itself.

Finally, suppose that two or three decades have passed, by which time the newly built office block will have declined into obsolescence, and consider whether the façade which has been propped up at such expense (it is an expensive process, even if profitable) is going to be worth preserving a second time round. What then will be the historical significance of such a paper-thin and heavily altered relic? Perhaps its real importance to future generations will be as a document of our own time and its unaccountable ways!

To be fair, few such completely destructive schemes make headway today, but some do – and many are permitted which do not fall far short of the extreme. Sometimes the front rooms only are retained to preserve an illusion of cellularity, sometimes a building is retained to its full depth but without a genuinely independent existence, its fate being inextricably tied

9.4a An American example of another fine masonry façade preserved by incorporation into a new and, in this case, much taller building. An expensive and, at first sight, generous homage to the past. But given the relatively short life now expected of such commercial developments, one wonders whether this thin layer (it is nothing more) will be thought worth the expense of holding up for a second time.

9.4b St Mary-at-Hill, City of London. Preservation celebrating total loss: The idea that the interest of an old building lies in its detachable 'features' can lead to this kind of collage, in which a new building is decorated with painful little souvenirs of the one that has been destroyed. These two finely carved corbels enriched a once handsome Victorian commercial building. Preserved in this fashion they are reduced to irrelevant bits of stone.

to that of a larger, alien – and relatively unadaptable – structure. All such 'skin-deep' projects are open to the kind of questioning suggested here.

Can we, then, say that façade preservation is never acceptable? Perhaps we should never say never. I can think of a few cases where it has been done without significant architectural loss and with such skill that it would take a keen observer – and a determined penetration of the building – to be aware that anything had happened. There are occasions when the careful preservation of the external appearance of a building (note the change of emphasis – and think about it) is preferable to total loss. This may particularly be the case where the building is unlisted but important in the streetscape, or where the interior is, as a matter of undeniable fact, either absent or utterly beyond saving.

Nevertheless, before contemplating such an approach the reader is recommended to look at some of the better known examples and ask how far one can really go in this direction and claim to be preserving anything worth while.

Three examples in particular illustrate the problems and pitfalls. An old house in Hereford now exists only as a two-dimensional timber-framed front, stuck on to the bland brick façade of a modern chain store, like a pictorial stamp on the corner of a plain envelope. The nature of the building is denied (timber frames do not have façades; the internal and external structures are completely integrated and inseparable) and its historical setting is utterly destroyed. If the modern building were to be deprived of its bit of timber framing, the fact would hardly be noticed. If the timber frame were to be deprived of the modern building it would fall over.

The old Royal Bank of Scotland in Princes Street, Edinburgh, is one of the most extreme examples of its kind to be seen anywhere. Its palazzo façade of 1888 is set against a glass curtain wall of 1976, which extends out to its left and also stands higher by one and a half storeys. The old bank quite clearly no longer forms part of an independent building of its own or any other period. It has no architectural kinship with the building it is attached to, which itself ostentatiously disregards what is left of the solid continuity of Princes Street. The retained façade could quite reasonably be interpreted as an accidentally surviving masonry wall, awaiting demolition so that the modern front can be completed.

I am told that some people regard the 'tension' set up by this extraordinary juxtaposition as architecturally exciting. If this is so, then there may be justification for it as an example of architectural inventiveness that just happens to have made use of an *objet trouvé*. It was, however, represented as an act of architectural conservation.

Thirdly, the highly praised Coutt's Bank Triangle at Charing Cross, London, needs more searching appraisal. As now seen, it undoubtedly offers new architectural pleasures but I doubt whether such radical treatment of a John Nash design, the stucco-faced West Strand Improvements of 1830, would have been permitted if the strategic planning authority had not already sold the pass by designing a road (happily never built) to cut right across the triangular site!

The slightly emphasised central block had already been rebuilt in 1903, in stone but using an architectural language not unrelated to, if rather less reserved than, that used by Nash. After total gutting and rebuilding within the triangle, two faces have now been given 're-created' Nash centres, but on the third side (facing the Strand) the 1903 centre section has been replaced by a recessed glass curtain wall, reversing the original architectural intention and creating a gap where previously there had been an architectural emphasis. A glass mansard slope rises above the curtain wall. The slope then continues at the same angle, but with lead facing, above the stuccoed façades on either side, raising immediate doubts about the nature of the building hiding behind the old walls. Looking into the central transparency to discover precisely what has happened, one sees a majestic space, the height of the whole building, architecturally unrelated to the Nash exterior. The façades themselves, with their short returns reflected in the new glass wall, produce the confusing effect of a Regency terrace only a few metres deep.

Whilst it is an interesting intellectual exercise to analyse in this way what has happened to a particular historic building (and a great deal more really needs to be said), it is done here simply to draw attention to the illogicalities and philosophical gymnastics which inevitably follow from the more extreme forms of recycling. Once the decision has been taken to indulge in, or to permit, this kind of radical approach, there is very little point in trying to construct a justification for it in building conservation terms. All that has been conserved is some sort of continuity in the townscape (certainly worth having) and a largish part of one attribute, the external design, of an old building. Even this has been reduced to a sort of deep cummerbund extending nearly, but not quite, around the perimeter of the site.

The Coutt's Triangle must now be judged principally as a creation of the late 1970s and, seen in that light, it is a striking work of its time, worthy of serious critical appraisal. From the viewpoint of this study, however, we can only say that what has happened is better than total loss – and we should consider whether the Nash buildings did not deserve more conservative treatment.

Skin-deep preservation
The Coutt's Bank Triangle, West Strand, London.
A particularly interesting example of recycling; essentially a work of architecture of the 1970s, incorporating a veneer of early nineteenth-century fabric.

9.5a Before gutting,

9.5b ... during gutting,

9.5c (above) … after gutting,

9.5d (left) detail.

Following the advice given earlier, if we ask ourselves (asking the building owner may produce a somewhat biased answer) 'Is this degree of disturbance actually necessary to save the life of the building?' the answer in all three cases described above – and a great many others – would almost certainly be 'No'. Even where the economic pressures are extreme (where, for example, the earning capacity of the building would be multiplied several-fold by reconstructing the floors to take higher loads) the honest answer will still often be 'No'. The desire to bring a building up to a performance standard it cannot reasonably achieve, in order to adapt it for a use it is unsuited for, is, as we have noted before, not in itself a good reason for launching an attack on its integrity and inherent adaptability.

Even in those cases where the answer has to be 'Yes' – perhaps because the internal structure has suffered extensive and extreme damage – we should still ask how little, rather than how much, reconstruction is justified in order to secure the building's structural and architectural health and return it to economic occupation.

Historic buildings are, by definition, survivors, and one important reason for survival is the fact that, on the whole, cellular, more or less flexible structures, assembled from small components made of long-available materials (wood, stone, burnt clay, lime, etc) and with relatively short-span floors, roofs and wall openings, have proved to be adaptable and resilient. Modern long-span buildings, rigidly structured in non-traditional materials, have shown themselves to be rather less so. All antiquarian considerations aside, it is unsafe to assume that substituting the latter form of construction for the former is a recipe for long life.

Let us assume, however, that a case has arisen where the condition of the building and every other environmental and economic circumstance surrounding it, make it so difficult to keep anything at all that the preservation of the external appearance alone seems to be the only practicable option. Accept, for the sake of argument, that this is going to mean attaching the old façade to a completely modern structure. Having settled for so little, is there really much point in insisting on the original walls being propped up while the new building works are in progress? It would be cheaper to dismantle and rebuild them, reusing as much of the old materials as possible. But if we do that, do we really need to keep any of the old pieces for the sake of historical authenticity?

Surely, now that we have decided that the original design is all that matters, it would be more sensible to copy it faithfully in sparkling new material, would it not? And if the building is all new, or nearly so, what is the point of being pernickety about such insignificant matters as the roof pitch? A steeper slope and a few feet extra in overall height would create some really useful space – and while we are about it, why not … etcetera, etcetera.

Constructing a conservationist case for large-scale destruction requires philosophical agility of a quite unnerving order – or an admission that what is being attempted may turn out to be more akin to stage design than building conservation. That does not necessarily make it invalid. It does move it to the farthest fringes of our concerns. The questions raised regarding the acceptability of renewal, reconstruction and reproduction are, nevertheless, of general relevance and will be examined next.

Repair and replacement

The questions which have to be dealt with are of a most intricate nature, always involving the consideration of the twin needs of structural stability and of conservation and sometimes also the making of alterations. In the course of work on an ancient building points difficult to decide and needing instant decision constantly arise. What needs renewal? How much may be retained? What technical method should be employed? and like questions confront one at every turn.
A R Powys, *Repair of Ancient Buildings*, 1929

Simple repair should, one might reasonably suppose, be a containable and uncontroversial subject. If a repair is limited to what is actually necessary to maintain the health of the fabric and if the techniques and materials required are all in common currency, there should not be too much philosophical stress in the air (the question of whether repairs should be visible or invisible will be dealt with later). Even where more unusual skills and materials are involved (perhaps cob, wattle and daub, mathematical tiling or flintwork), provided they can actually be obtained in adequate quality and quantity, then common sense and the practical insights of craftsmen can be effective guides – subject, of course, to the craftsmen actually possessing and not merely claiming expertise.

What must be done in practical terms can rarely be wrong in philosophical terms. The question of 'what must be done' nevertheless clearly requires judgment. The more experienced and sensitive the practitioner, the less likely are the judgments to be challenged. If the social conditions and traditions which produced the building are still flourishing (a not uncommon situation in some parts of the world – and not utterly impossible in Britain where more recent buildings are concerned), the question of refined judgment hardly arises, since the repairer should, as a matter of habit, incline to the right course. This takes us back to the beginning of Chapter 3 and the statement that 'at its simplest, preservation is synonymous with prudent maintenance'.

Faulty judgments arise from ignorance of the availability of crafts and materials, the desire to find cheap and easy solutions and the belief that modern methods are, in any case, superior to traditional methods. The ingrained idea that a proper job necessarily involves extensive works is a particularly dangerous kind of ignorance, invariably dressed up as wisdom.

All of these factors (and they commonly occur in combination) can lead to devastation in the name of repair – and the consequences are not always obvious before the event. Readers know from instruction, if not experience, that cob walls can be destroyed by ill-advised repair, and that the use of cement-rich mortars can damage brick and stonework. But what about interferences which seem at first sight desirable and leave no obvious trace? For example, the insertion of damp-proofing membranes may upset stable conditions and cause deterioration in quite unexpected ways. Before accepting that, say, dampness in a wall is a condition to be 'cured' by standard procedures, it is wise to ask oneself why things are as they are and then seek solutions that work with rather than against the nature of the building.

One very real problem is that the conservation needs of a building do not always fit snugly with commonly accepted maintenance principles. When dealing with an historic building we are concerned not only with the aesthetic acceptability of repairs (see Chapter 7, 'Matters of choice') but also with the authenticity of the old fabric and, therefore, with limiting change to what is absolutely necessary. Conservation is very largely the art of controlling change.

Received preventive maintenance wisdom may suggest that the time has come to renew all the wooden sash windows in a building. Let us say that several have rot in their cills, bottom rails and box frames, most have become ill fitting and some have been repaired in an unsightly manner in the past. The total renewal of a dozen or more, all in careful reproduction of the original design, will be much cheaper than renewing one or two at a time and will produce a smart, completely uniform effect – surely what the original architect or builder intended? Disruption will be limited to the few days taken to remove the old windows and install the factory-made replacements. Future maintenance costs will be much reduced, at least for the next twenty or thirty years.

Repair, by contrast, will be expensive, slow and never-ending. It will call for high quality craftsmen employed on the site, interfering, room by room, with the use of the building. There will never be a crisp 'as-new' uniformity in appearance.

Continuous repair sounds like a poor deal. We must, nevertheless, opt for it. The old sash windows, for all their visible wear and tear, are authentic. If we are preserving the building for what it is, for what it represents and for what it can tell us about its time, they are not disposable. They are part of the original design and still contain much original material, contributing to what Ruskin called 'some life, some mysterious suggestion of what [the building] had once been ... some sweetness in the general lines' which we respond to in the old and which cannot be present in the new. Some new work there will have to be, but let it be limited to what is actually necessary. The craftsman working on the site will take pride in retaining the old glass (quite different from modern glass), servicing and refixing the old ironmongery and brassware and even arguing over the appropriateness of using flax lines and lead weights. The glass, the fasteners, pulleys and weights would all have finished up in the skip with a total renewal job. Ageing and dissolution can never be completely eliminated, but a continuous process of overhaul is, from the viewpoint of conservation, a more natural and far less destructive process than periodic renewal campaigns.

Some repairs that occur only at very long intervals are of their nature extensive, unavoidably introducing a great deal of new material. A lead roof which has got beyond repair by lead burning cannot reasonably be replaced a bay at a time over a period of years, neither can the decay of a stained glass window be tackled otherwise than by complete releading. At another level, protective repainting, which obscures if it does not destroy all trace of earlier paint layers, must take place at relatively short intervals. In all such cases, the logic of conservation demands continuity of material and craft traditions. For the least specialised of observers, the pleasurable sensation of communication with the past is destroyed if, for example, a perfectly preserved public room (a council chamber, ballroom or theatre, perhaps) reflects in an aggressive way the decorative tastes and finishes of our own time.

It may be necessary for the health of the building to make tactful amendments to original detail (a lead roof, for instance, may have been laid in oversized bays, leading to fatigue) but it must be realised that every departure from former practice to some extent vitiates the record. Cases can also arise where a detail that has proved to be self-destructive was devised for architectural reasons (some kinds of secret gutter fall into this category) so that any change is bound to modify the original architectural conception. One can only strive in such instances to produce a discreet solution.

Care must, in any case, always be taken to examine the possible consequences of seemingly harmless corrective works which actually introduce new risks, such as the impairment of natural ventilation routes.

The temptation to substitute milled lead (or something altogether cheaper) for cast lead, or to use the latest thing in high gloss or textured 'protective' paints or to make any other change for the sake of economy or supposedly better performance should often be resisted for practical as well as philosophical reasons. Before determining on any such steps in order to 'save' a building, it is a good idea to consider how it has achieved longevity without such aids.

Restoration and reproduction

Valid arguments both for and against the restoration of old buildings can always be found. But each case has to be judged on its own merits, the most important axiom being that whatever work is done is in competent and sympathetic hands. There is, however, a great difference between necessary repair and faithful reinstatement of hopelessly worn out parts on the one hand and 'restoration' to something purely conjectural on the other.
Peter Fleetwood Hesketh, 'A Watchdog of Preservation', *Country Life*, March 1967

The tendency to be over-energetic in repair is akin to, and often goes hand-in-hand with, the desire for restoration or (in view of the fact that the word 'restoration' now tends to be used as a synonym for tender loving care – a usage which would have been impossible a century ago) we should perhaps say 'over-restoration'.

Over-restoration is of regrettably frequent occurrence amongst home owners who believe that every penny spent on the beautification of their treasured properties must be beneficial. In the commercial property world it certainly has chequebook appeal. Who wants to see a plain nineteenth-century replacement staircase in an imposing eighteenth-century town house (now commanding a high price per metre as offices) when, with imagination and as little research as will help to shore up your case, you can make a stab at the kind of staircase it very possibly once had?

Regarding more cautious and scholarly reinstatements (the word is carefully chosen), opinions differ, even amongst acknowledged experts – even amongst those who have the SPAB *Manifesto* engraved on their hearts.

This is yet another area where it is dangerous to lay down firm rules, but consider the following.

All buildings which survive for a long time are likely to suffer alteration. Sometimes alterations are of such interest in their own right as to claim an absolute right for preservation, if only as evidence of the changing life history of the building. Others, regardless of when they were carried out, are mindless mutilations of no value except as proof that the building has been through a period when it was held in low regard. There are, of course, shades of interest between the two extremes – and we should not overlook the fact that some changes may have been made for the very good reason that the original work was faultily detailed and self-destructive. We should also beware of dismissing as a mutilation a perfectly civilised alteration or addition which simply happens to be currently unfashionable.

For the sake of this argument, set aside the small number of rare and fragile buildings, usually of great antiquity, where any intervention beyond simple protection must be approached with extreme reluctance.

In most cases it should not be too difficult to distinguish between destructive restoration or unnecessary repair, and unarguably desirable reinstatement. There need to be very pressing reasons to justify the knocking down of a decently designed and potentially useful old addition to an earlier building; but, equally, no building should continue to suffer a mutilation which has seriously damaged its integrity and added nothing of interest or utility. The fact that such a mutilation has survived for a lifetime rather than a few unhappy years does not increase its claims for recognition. Where the principal interest of a building resides in its architectural design it can rarely be wrong to replace missing elements, provided it can be done with absolute certainty (look at the pictures of Hackney Empire on the English Heritage leaflet *Principles of Repair*) and without loss of authentic fabric.

SPAB philosophy would limit reinstatement to what is necessary for practical and structural, rather than aesthetic reasons, but many sensitive practitioners have made reasonable departures from this rather hard rule. If the crowning balustrade on a grand façade suffers neglect and part of it falls down, it should be repaired and the gaps made good. If the whole thing was ignorantly destroyed fifty years ago to reduce maintenance costs, should it not be replaced as a simple matter of regrettably deferred maintenance? Following the total loss of an architectural feature, irrefutable evidence for reconstruction may be a little harder to come by than in a case where only partial renewal is needed, but by studying the building itself, together with old drawings, photographs and such remnants as can be found by searching the ground for rubbish (it is surprising how often this can be productive), the design can usually be recovered.

Where reinstatement is clearly the right course, there must be careful attention to every detail of architectural and craft vocabulary, however small. Having regard to the 'spirit' of the original is not good enough. There can be no justification for the exercise at all if the moulding profiles, glazing bar sections and brick dimensions (to select only three items vital to the character of one kind of design) are not consonant with those originally employed. But it should be noted that this kind of reinstatement, even when based on supposedly unimpeachable evidence, is not completely free from risk. I have seen missing room panelling replaced by reference to the surviving panelled walls, reproducing the moulding profiles faithfully – and expensively – from thickly painted originals. Some future conserver is in for a surprise if it ever becomes necessary to strip the paint in this room, since three walls will be found to have razor-sharp profiles, drawn 'from the book', whilst the fourth will display a suite of soft, sausagey shapes!

Looking back, for a moment, to the section on 'Repair and replacement', the ruinous state of some large part of a building may become so advanced that – however much the fact may be regretted – only thoroughgoing reconstruction will cope with the problem. The same situation can arise after serious fire, flood or earthquake damage. Such a reconstruction amounts to a major trauma. Certainly, in Ruskin's terms, the life and mystery of the old will be lost, even if we protest that a faithful reproduction will not be 'a lie from beginning to end'. If radical intervention of this kind is unavoidable, then it must be done in as sensitive and truthful a way as possible (see below for a discussion of matching and non-matching work).

In many cases there is, in fact, no point in reconstruction (unless for purely utilitarian or symbolic reasons) since the interest of the crumbling and perhaps fragmentary structure resided wholly in the authenticity of its fabric. In some cases, for example the reconstruction of a great barn using much of the old salvaged timber, there may be an act of piety involved. The awesome effect of re-erected mediaeval trusses has been seen to sweep away philosophical objections – demonstrating that conservation can be an emotive as well as a scholarly business. The most extreme and striking manifestations of piety and patriotism can be seen in the reconstructions of ruined buildings in Flanders and Northern France after World War I and the total recreations in Warsaw after World War II. What was done there cannot be described as building conservation – it is as far from it as Viollet-le-Duc's campaigns of emendation – but we should not lose sight of the fact that the desire to recover the past will still surface from time to time and cannot easily be brushed aside. Who would dare to say that the people of Warsaw were wrong to heal their wounds in this way?

Philosophical problems should be rather less severe when a building which is a great work of art is subjected to unavoidable partial reconstruction. The fact that what we see today in the Whitehall façade of Inigo Jones's Banqueting House of 1619 is entirely the result of a refacing by Sir John Soane (210 years later, in a different stone) does not invalidate it as an historic monument. It remains the creation of Jones's genius. Perhaps today a less drastic repair would have been attempted, but the decision might not, even now, be clear-cut.

The Banqueting House was a revolutionary and quite astonishing arrival on the architectural scene that must have produced a far greater shock to the sensibilities of cultured people than the Lloyd's building does today. This is one of the most important facts about it. It would, in my opinion, have been wrong (and by now the reader should be able to argue the opposing case) to allow such a crucial monument to decay to the point where its details were unreadable and the purity and perfection of the design lost. It would be immensely more exciting to see Inigo Jones's façade as he first saw it, if that were possible – but since it is not, then Soane has at least given us a very satisfactory 'next best' transmission of Jones's revolutionary architectural message. An Australian, referring for guidance to the *Burra Charter* (see Appendix 4), would have little trouble in identifying Jones's design as the most 'culturally significant' part of the building's history and identity. Although that charter was drafted to deal with the special problems of conservation in Australia, I suggest that this approach can have wider validity.

This is not, of course, to say that a work of architecture should ever be unnecessarily subject to massive intervention. It is simply a fact that architecture can, to an extent and if circumstances dictate, be translated into building at a distance in time after the original design has been made. For reasons we have already examined, architectural designs are not to be picked up and used anywhere, without regard to their structural and other implications, but they do have a kind of hardiness which buildings themselves lack. It would, for example, be perfectly possible to rebuild the wantonly destroyed Euston Arch in new material with complete accuracy (and I may say that I would rejoice in such a symbolic penance) but in conservation terms the recreation of a design can only make sense if there is a great deal of saveable fabric already in existence and *in situ*. Even then, the risk of slipping into an interesting and subversive game of conjecture is ever present. It makes less sense in conservation terms (although it may be desired for a variety of aesthetic and town planning reasons) to attempt extensive reconstruction where the original building is the product of a pattern book or craft tradition.

An extraordinary example of rebuilding from an original design, nearly a decade after demolition, can be seen at the Lyric Theatre Hammersmith. The old Lyric of 1895 was torn down to make way for a rather uninspired town centre development. Demolition was permitted, subject to a record being made and moulds and patterns being taken. The prospect that they might be used to create a new theatre seemed remote at the time, but in 1979 a theatre was created at a short distance from its original site and well above ground level within a new block. The 1895 auditorium design was repeated but to cope with modern production requirements, the proscenium opening was enlarged and this, in turn, led to practically every other dimension having to be stretched. The enlargement was done almost invisibly, employing the original design vocabulary and the re-creation is architecturally satisfying, but the appearance of an elaborate Victorian rococo interior within a completly modern building is inclined to produce gasps of surprise. There is not much point in arguing over whether the Lyric is an example of acceptable conservation practice. It is surprising that so much as a memory of the original design was rescued from the rubble.

Returning to the matter of reinstatement of missing or mutilated elements or components, we have to consider what to do when something is clearly missing, its original character is not known with certainty and assiduous research has failed to produce the knowledge. Speculative restoration and flights of creative fancy cannot be justified. There can, nevertheless, be a case for doing something rather than nothing in cases where the absence of a particular feature is putting a building physically at risk, or has a particularly unsightly effect, perhaps even deterring possible users. Even then, the design problems involved are so testing that experienced conservation practices may feel the need to call for an opinion from experts in the architecture of the period in question before determining on this course of action.

Substitute materials

The use of modern substitute materials has already been touched on above, but the same question frequently arises where an ornamental component is clearly beyond repair and its reinstatement will be extremely expensive. The best advice to be offered in such cases is 'be on your guard'. Few substitutes are ever really quite that. A close resemblance in initial appearance does not imply that performance will be identical or even closely comparable.

Temptation arises most often where there is a genuine choice (it is more often a false choice, driven by the 'later is better as well as cheaper' fallacy) between having the feature reinstated in substitute material or not having it at all.

One favourite, GRP (Glass Reinforced Plastic), has performed well in situations where reproduced decorative elements can be painted (for example on stucco façades). The fact that it is cheaper in repetition has, however, led to the unnecessary renewal of, for example, perfectly sound carved eaves brackets along with a few rotted ones, robbing a building of authentic features, depriving a wood carver of continuity of work and giving the developer (it is usually a developer) less assurance of longevity than the original material would have given. The loss of fabric is, in conservation terms, unjustifiable. The argument that the building benefits by having the risk of rot removed is not supportable even in purely economic terms since, although the durability of the old material has been demonstrated, the long-term performance of the new has still to be proved. In very exposed positions (such as spires and finials) and in unpainted (self-colour) states, there is some evidence to show that GRP is not a suitably durable replacement for lead, stone or terracotta, even in the medium term.

The argument that modern substitutes (for our present purpose we have no need to look at them all) must be acceptable where the original material was itself a substitute – that Nash and Burton were using stucco or patent mastic to represent Bath stone and would have been delighted to use the vastly superior GRXYZ (my own patent) if it had been available – is utterly unconvincing. Apart from the fact that there is something slightly absurd in the thought of a building faced with GRXYZ masquerading as stucco masquerading as Bath stone, a building is surely a candidate for preservation because it is of its time, and because it is built in the manner of that time. We cannot know whether early nineteenth-century architects would have been excited or repelled by modern rooflights or uPVC casements and the question is, in fact, irrelevant. No such choice existed for them.

As conservers of old buildings we are better employed in studying how the buildings we are dealing with were made, and prescribing treatments which make use of those long-tested materials and techniques which are most in harmony with what exists.

Restoration by unravelling

A particularly difficult case to deal with occurs where a building of great architectural distinction has been altered or extended at some stage so that the finished effect, although not completely without interest in its own right, obscures much more important earlier work. In these circumstances the spirit of the nineteenth-century restorer will frequently surface and generate much the same kind of controversy as occurred in the earliest days of Anti-Scrape. The consensus represented by such documents as the *Venice Charter* notwithstanding, this argument is likely to go on forever. I advise the reader to be aware of the issues as they manifest themselves today – and be ready to answer the criticism that unravelling the past to recover formerly existing perfection is not much better than Viollet-le-Duc's 'restorations' to formerly unachieved perfection.

One thing is certain. Destruction in the name of restoration is irreversible. Look, however, at what was done to Marble Hill in Twickenham. This beautiful Palladian villa of 1724–29 was altered and extended in the 1820s but restored to its original design in 1965–66, demolishing the later additions and returning windows and other features to their original form.

Turning to the *Venice Charter*, we read:

> *The valid contributions of all periods to the building of a monument must be respected, since unity of style is not the aim of restoration. When a building includes the superimposed work of different periods, the revealing of the underlying state can only be justified in exceptional circumstances and when what is removed is of little interest and the material which is brought to light is of great historical, archaeological or aesthetic value and its state of preservation good enough to justify the action.*
> Venice Charter, Article 11, 1964.

Faced with a specific case, the second sentence, with its four conditional clauses, leaves some room for argument. In the end, a nicely balanced judgment is involved. For many, the presence of a perfect textbook Palladian villa on the Thames which, before 1965, could be appreciated only in

9.6a Perfection regained? Marble Hill, Twickenham before restoration *(Reproduced by permission of London Metropolitan Archives)*

9.6b (below) … after restoration. *(Reproduced by permission of London Metropolitan Archives)*

engravings, justifies a relatively small balancing loss. Few voices are now heard wishing Marble Hill back to its pre-restoration form.

One further case of wholesale intervention illustrates, quite literally in black and white, the inescapable philosophical problems which flow from attempts to restore a building to a former state.

No. 17 Fleet Street, London, existed in 1900 as a much-altered relic of a timber-framed tavern of 1611 incorporating the Inner Temple gateway. Its casemented oriels had been cut back and a pilastered false front added, but the original storey posts survived *in situ*. On the first floor there was some original panelling and a fine ceiling incorporating the Prince of Wales's feathers, which gave the place its popular, but historically erroneous, name of 'Prince Henry's Room'.

When the building was acquired by the County Council in connection with the widening of Fleet Street, it was decided not to demolish it, but to adapt the ground floor to the new improvement line, strip off the nineteenth-century front and restore the upper floors to their original appearance. The restoration was based on evidence provided by investigation of the surviving parts together with research into documentary and illustrative sources – and a degree of conjecture.

The resulting twin-gabled, jettied front, as completed in 1903–16 by the London County Council architects, was described by Sir Nikolaus Pevsner as 'one of the best pieces of half-timber work in London' (*Buildings of England: London* (City and Westminster) 1957). The words are literally true. What is actually seen, however, is a reconstructed ground floor, no longer in exact relationship to the timber framing above, which is itself more than fifty percent new. The casements are new, the gallery is new and the gables have been completely remade.

The restoration was carried out with genuine reverence and skill. The architects who worked on it were, in fact, early members of the SPAB. It is as correct as the scholarship of the time could make it, it is more than skin-deep and it is extremely satisfying as an 'event' in the London scene. If less sensitive minds had been at work there would have been a demolition rather than a restoration. Can the result, nevertheless, be justified in building conservation terms?

Minds may be usefully exercised in proposing and analysing the philosophical arguments for and against – but there is no need to be judgmental about this case. It belongs to history and is now, in itself, a splendid example of an approach to conservation which, although open to question in its day, must be regarded as sensitive and serious.

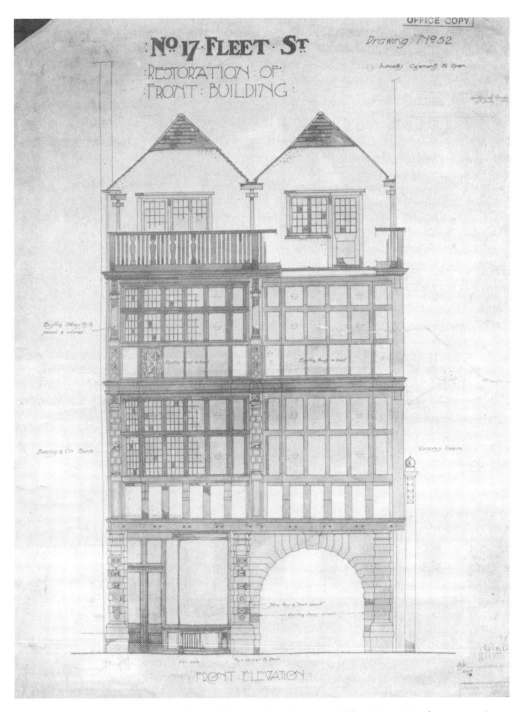

9.7a Loving care and a minimum of conjecture; 17 Fleet Street, London restoration drawing dated 1903 *(Reproduced by permission of London Metropolitan Archives)*

9.7b 17 Fleet Street, London …before restoration *(Reproduced by permission of London Metropolitan Archives)*

9.7c 17 Fleet Street … after restoration.

As an aside (and to some extent a warning, relevant to 'Additions' below) the rear parts of this building were described in 1900 as 'uninteresting' (meaning post-Queen Anne) and totally rebuilt in a charming Arts and Crafts-inspired manner similar to that employed by the young LCC housing architects of the time. The best of their work is now admired and listed; so is 'uninteresting' plain Georgian fabric of the kind they demolished.

As a final thought under this heading: however well justified an intervention may be, all major campaigns of repair, reconstruction or demolition should be seen as non-recurring opportunities for investigation, research and recording. This will be touched on again later.

Visible or invisible?

Debate over the question of whether repairs and other works (for additions, see below) should be visible or invisible to the inexpert eye can generate a surprising amount of heat. As I have done with other controversial matters, I will take in alternative views, indicating where, in my opinion, common sense should lead us, but inviting the reader to examine as many cases as possible and to beware of adopting a dogmatic position.

The general rule that the work of modern hands should be clearly seen, so as not to confuse the historical record or dilute the authenticity of the original fabric, is so reasonable as to invite instant adoption. If a building is being preserved because of its antiquity, its rarity, its historical, architectural and artistic significance, its associations, singular construction, fine craftsmanship or any combination of such reasons, then authenticity is of prime importance. We may reasonably feel cheated and robbed if we discover that the mellow old brickwork we have been admiring actually dates from 1950 and has been artificially aged – or that a splendidly 'restored' panelled study is actually a concoction of old pieces of dubious provenance from an architectural salvage store.

The building, then, should tell a true story. I do, however, sometimes wonder whether it is really necessary to shout the truth from the housetops. Aggressively visible repairs can distract attention from the very qualities that mark out a building for preservation. A little discretion may be no bad thing.

Interestingly, insistence on super-honesty usually comes from those scholars and conservation specialists who are least likely to be fooled by sleight of hand. However, having been taken in myself, at least for a while, by some skilful forgeries, I am sensitive to the risk that one may misread the record, draw wrong conclusions or make erroneous attributions.

For example: many quite knowledgeable observers would assume without investigation that the preserved façade (it is now nothing more) of Schomberg House in Pall Mall dates entirely from 1698. One projecting wing is, in fact, of recent date, a total re-creation after a cruel nineteenth-century partial redevelopment. It seems to me that the recovery of the original symmetry had a lot to be said for it architecturally and I am certainly more appalled by the alien nature of the building behind the façade than by what has happened to the façade itself – but anyone who cares for historical truth as well as appearances must feel uneasy about this amazingly convincing reproduction. If the innards of the house, or some recognisable remnant of it, had survived and if the reproduction had been just a bit

9.8a Repair: the work of modern hands should be discreet but detectable, not crude and offensive. Mediaeval masonry damaged and defaced by incompetent modern pointing.

9.8b (below) Where weathering is severe the most expert repair can be distressingly obvious.

more obvious, the charge that Schomberg House is now little more than stage scenery would be harder to make stick.

This kind of exploitation of historic fabric can only be represented as building conservation in the commercial development context in which it usually occurs – the argument being that, since it is highly skilled work which does not involve total demolition, it must be conservation. It is usually spectacular in its way, but inexcusable in genuine conservation terms – and not particularly relevant to the issue under examination. Our concern here is with whether an unarguably necessary repair or replacement should be immediately detectable or not.

It is, in fact, quite difficult to deceive the eye of the expert without deliberately setting out to create a blatant forgery – and it is not easy even then. New work has a way of being inescapably of its own time. However skilled the craftsman and however neatly the new and the old are melded together, there will be visible differences which are neither to be regretted nor concealed. To strive for deliberate concealment is to play a quite unnecessary and usually highly undesirable game of deception, but to accentuate those differences and produce a situation where the lay observer asks questions about the repair rather than the repaired is surely just as undesirable. The ideal repair/replacement, in my view, is one that the expert can detect fairly quickly and the inexpert will see when attention has been drawn to it.

Interesting problems arise where new work has to be inserted into badly weathered, worn or obscured original fabric. I have already touched on this in connection with an incomplete panelled room with mouldings thick with paint but a more difficult case is one where profiles have eroded away, especially on external stonework. Should the new work be faithful to the original design, so that the profiles stand out from the surface of the weathered original work? Any compromise (by introducing, for example, softened forms) will be a misrepresentation. But the strictly honest 'new and sharp' replacement, representing a single step on the long road to progressive total replacement, can be quite startlingly ugly – and there can never be a moment when the distressingly new, the partly weathered 'old new' and the original (or 'old old') present a completely integrated appearance.

Once again, there is no right-every-time solution on offer. It must be accepted that repair which eschews deliberate and radical restoration cannot in any case turn back the clock. A preserved building can never quite be what it once was. We come back every time to the question of motive. If the link with the past is tied up so completely with a precious original fabric that even slight losses cannot be contemplated without extreme misgiving, then the best we can hope for is to slow the processes of erosion. The new work can be no more than a connecting tissue, frankly and obviously inserted to extend the life of the irreplaceable. If the architectural design, on the other hand, is of supreme importance and the materials and crafts used in its realisation are still current, aesthetic judgment as well as practical imperatives will reasonably colour decisions. In such cases it may be possible to exercise a little more choice as to the precise point where new work meets old, in order to make a repair less visually disturbing. When judgments of this kind have to be made it is invariably safer to err on the side of restraint and to bear in mind that deliberate attempts to mislead – by introducing artificial weathering and soiling, for example – are opposed to the fundamental purposes of conservation.

Mention of soiling prompts a note on cleaning. It is often thought to be (less often is) advisable to clean a building in order to make contrasting new material less obvious. This, again, is very much a matter for judgment, but a general caveat can be issued. Gentle cleaning (fairly obviously) removes surface soiling and may slow down some kinds of chemical attack and erosion, but it is a mistake to suppose that it can return the old fabric to the appearance it had when new. By contrast, harsher cleaning methods, nearly always preferred by commercial recyclers of old buildings, can produce an illusion of brilliance and renewed youth but nearly always result in a condition that bears no relation to any former or even credibly natural state. Worse than this, the scouring of brickwork or terracotta, for example, by sand-blasting, can destroy the surface and actually accelerate the processes of dissolution – especially if, as commonly occurs, the devastated mortar joints are immediately subjected to inexpert repointing.

Second-hand materials, the demand for which, incidentally, has turned many a serviceable old building into a quarry for the heritage trade, can be as dangerous a seduction as modern substitutes. On occasions (repairs to some kinds of roof coverings can be a case in point) they may produce a completely acceptable result, but more often the effect is unhappy. Second-hand bricks, for example, have usually suffered a multitude of little knocks in the processes of demolition, cleaning and transportation. Even if from the same original source as those in the wall to be repaired, they invariably look less well preserved than the undisturbed bricks and may produce a much less visually satisfactory repair than one carried out with well-matched new bricks. The practice of building whole new structures of second-hand bricks in order to 'be in keeping' with their genuinely old neighbours can produce a very odd effect indeed. The best that can be said about such brickwork is that it will always be recognisably of its own time, since no earlier wall could ever have looked like that!

Unseen structure

The preservation of unseen structure can be dealt with in a few words. Invisible does not mean unimportant. Just as the exterior of a building gives rise to expectations about its interior, so do its visible forms speak, however discreetly, of the nature of its construction. If we are preserving a building for what it tells us about itself and its time, it does not make much sense to destroy a vital part of its message.

The fact that there is no obvious daily delight to be had from, say, the concealed construction of an old roof is neither here nor there. The mighty timbers above the stone vaulting of a cathedral are seen by relatively few, but they are nonetheless part of a precious inheritance to be studied, cared for, and only under pressure of direst need replaced by modern fabric.

Even on a strictly practical level it is never quite safe to assume that we know so much about a complex building that we can safely replace an old structural system with a completely new and different apparatus of support without setting off a train of unexpected consequences, some of which may become apparent only after the passage of years. And even if the replacement could be made without risk, there is a fundamental issue of historical truth to consider.

Ordinarily sensitive people, as well as scholars, can feel that a building has been seriously devalued by the kind of taxidermy which preserves (or appears to preserve) the skin whilst discarding the skeleton.

It is usually sound practice as well as philosophically desirable to treat the visible and the invisible alike, limiting intervention to what is actually essential and making repairs in a manner compatible with the existing structural forms and materials.

Change of use

This, too, can be considered briefly, since the essential point was made concisely in 1987 in an official Circular.

> *The best use for an historic building is obviously the use for which it was designed and wherever possible this original use ... should continue. If the use ... has been changed from its original purpose, it should be considered whether it can revert to it.*
>
> *The greatest problems arise when large buildings, built for needs which have ceased to exist, become vacant ...*
> DoE *Circular 8/87*, Paras 20 and 21, on 'New Uses for Old Buildings'

This section of the old Circular (which goes on to consider the desirable and undesirable effects of change of use) might have added that aesthetic appeal can be materially diminished by unsuitable use.

The conversion of a fine industrial building to offices, for example, leading to its impressive internal spaces being subdivided and its slender iron columns solidly encased, damages the very qualities which recommended it for preservation. The original fabric may be intact and recoverable, but if it cannot be 'read' properly, public interest in its preservation can rapidly wane.

It may be necessary to accept works of this kind (provided they are reversible) if the true alternative is dereliction, but the dangers of visual degradation need to be recognised. The closer the new use corresponds to the designed use, the less severe the practical and aesthetic consequences are likely to be.

One possible consequence of radically changed use is dealt with in the following, final section of this chapter.

Additions

Extensive additions to historic buildings, no matter how carefully designed and executed, must to some degree interfere with appreciation of the thing preserved. If, however, a building is to survive in drastically changed circumstances, they may be hard to resist. The question then arises: Should the new construction be designed to appear as if it belonged to the same time as the original building or should it be sharply distinguished from it and be seen as a work of our own time?

Some of the relevant issues have already been looked at in relation to repair and reinstatement (see above) but a substantial extension which is attached to and becomes an inseparable part (perhaps even the larger part) of an older building presents special problems.

There are two main and almost directly opposed risks. The first is that the new will so successfully ape the old as to blur its individuality and confuse the historical record. The second is that the new will strive so hard to be distinguishable from the old that it will compete for attention with its neighbour. These risks relate to internal planning and design as well as external appearance, but internal transitions are probably, on the whole, easier to deal with.

An eighteenth-century visionary planner, one whose opinions are always worth considering, was in no doubt about the need for architectural consistency in any new work:

> *[The] custom of mixing Gothick and Modern architecture in the same*
> *pile of buildings has… been practised in the university of Oxford with*
> *great success and serves to shew that very little attention is paid to*
> *taste and elegance in places where one would expect to find hardly*
> *anything else. If these things are suffered to be done merely because*
> *they produce variety, they should be told that variety may be*
> *produced in Gothick architecture without changing the stile and that*
> *at the same time a harmony may be produced without destroying the*
> *connection of what is already built; in short, very great, noble and*
> *elegant things may be done in the Gothick taste and, with proper*
> *attention, not prove so expensive as may be imagined.*
> John Gwynn, *London and Westminster Improved*, 1766

'Great success' in Gwynn's first sentence seems to refer solely to the functionality of the new buildings, since he clearly regarded them as lacking in taste.

Modern policy statements, by contrast, tend to be unequivocal in requiring complete honesty:

> *A modest addition is not opposed to the principles of the Society*
> *provided … that the new work is in the natural manner of today,*
> *subordinate to the old and not a reproduction of any past style [and]*
> *… permanently required.*
> Note dated 1924 attached to the SPAB *Manifesto* – since deleted, but repeated
> here because it represents the view of many expert practitioners today.

> *Additions cannot be allowed except in so far as they do not detract*
> *from the interesting parts of the building, its traditional setting, the*
> *balance of its composition and its relation with its surroundings.*
> *Venice Charter*, Article 13, 1964

The first rule is, in practice, so restrictive that it is quite often stretched or even broken. There is also going to be more ferocious argument now than there was in 1924 over what constitutes 'the natural manner of today'. The second starts off in an uncompromising manner ('cannot be allowed') but, on close examination, leaves an acreage of space for interpretation in particular circumstances. Once again we have to say that we shall find no answers to suit all circumstances.

The fact is that such demanding design problems can no more be left in the hands of any architect than sensitive repair work can be left to any

9.9 Passions can be roused by almost any kind of substantial addition made to an historic building. It may be possible in some cases to complete an architectural intention: When Thomas Archer designed Roehampton House in 1712, he intended its symmetry to be completed by advanced wings and an enclosed courtyard. In 1913 Lutyens added handsome but rather more substantial wings than Archer intended, then in 1962, following a road widening, the London County Council built a gateway and a pair of lodges of Lutyensesque character.

9.10 The addition (the Sainsbury Wing) to the National Gallery is neither an extension in the same style, nor a sharply contrasting neighbour. Venturi adopted a policy of transition from Wilkins's expressed classical order, to an implied or 'incomplete' order, then to a plain modern treatment, but all executed in stone to match the original building.

maintenance surveyor. Despite the fact that, historically, the leading build-ing conservation experts have been architects, very few architects today complete their professional training with any useful grounding in conser-vation or conservation-related design. An architect engaged for this pur-pose must be one with a proven track record in subordinating his or her creative ambitions to the special needs of historic buildings. Such special-ists are in short supply and they tend not to be amongst the fashionable stars of the architectural world.

Whatever approach is adopted, we are more than likely to be faced with a variety of ready-made opinions – and not only those of clients and con-trolling authorities. The addition must be a very small and insignificant one not to attract attention from those who have fixed ideas (not necessar-ily arising from an examination of the facts) of what a building should look like. These ideas, the layman's view, for example, that a timber frame which is not black and white is wrong, or the architectural article of faith that anything newly built in traditional manner is an immoral fake, may be exasperating at times, but they must, nevertheless, be acknowledged in any explanation of the policy adopted in a particular case.

Where a well-known public building is involved, argument is likely to rage with particular fury between the interested lay public, resisting any-thing unfamiliar, and the architectural establishment, resisting anything unoriginal. The National Gallery extension was an interesting case in point, with both high-tech and highly conservative solutions being equally derided and abused by one side or the other, as ignorant, cowardly or heretical.

The conservation specialist, at least, should try to stand aside from such unseemly shouting matches and take a reasoned position. An extension should, surely, neither quarrel openly with the old building nor swamp it with 'miles more of the same'.

I suggest (and readers are urged not to accept my view but to look closely at relevant recent cases and argue the matter out for themselves) that satisfactory results have been achieved by working both within and without the architectural language of the parent building. Most successful solutions seem to me to suggest a common cultural ancestry, however dis-tant. They eschew fashionable mannerisms, techniques and finishes that will lose their novelty in a very short time and they leave attention firmly fixed on the old building.

The least satisfactory solutions are (I suggest) those which copy the existing building so closely as to amount to a rewriting of its history (completing an original architectural intention is another matter, even if

9.11a and b The way in which the uncompromisingly neo-classical theatre in Lyon has been added to in an equally uncompromisingly modern manner has raised many eyebrows. It must be said, however, that once the decision has been taken to increase the volume of a building to this degree by upward extension, the precise style adopted is almost immaterial. There is a limit of addition beyond which the original building (in this case, reduced to a containing shell) becomes the tail of an over-large dog.

open to the dreaded charge of 'the vandalism of completion'); or which mimic the general character of the original design, but crudifying it, with the excuse that the new work is thus identified as an honest creation 'of our time'. Equally unsatisfactory are those where the existing character is wilfully ignored on the grounds that to do anything else is morally unacceptable.

I have already remarked that argument as to whether new work is truly 'of our time' can be something of a red herring, and now offer the view that architectural morality is an even redder one. The term has no meaning until one's reflexes have been conditioned to apply a particular meaning to it – and the whole purpose of this study has been to promote thoughtful rather than reflexive judgements.

Readers should look at and examine their own reactions to such examples of major addition as the National Gallery (Venturi's 'slow-fade classic'), Lutyens's, and later the London County Council's completion (more or less) of Archer's unexecuted ideas for the forecourt of Roehampton House, Pei's pyramid at the Louvre (if you agree that this is an addition to an architectural ensemble), the 1968 entrance wing to York Theatre Royal and the extensive 1990s additions to the Royal Opera House complex. The last of these illustrates in an extreme form the kinds of compromises that may be presented where a building of outstanding architectural and historic importance is also an intensively worked technical apparatus (see cover illustrations).

When examining the last of these, look in particular at the old, formerly adjoining, Floral Hall, which has been totally reconstructed within the complex at higher level. Does the fact that the Floral Hall was, from the beginning, a prefabricated cast iron structure influence your judgement of what has been done?

Look also nearer home. There will almost certainly be an old church in your own neighbourhood which has been extended (perhaps after some argument as to the appropriate manner) to provide, for example, a new community room. Has any harm been done to the architectural, historic and archaeological interest (don't forget this last aspect) of the church? Is the extension the first thing you see or the last thing you notice? And, if you find the solution adopted is in any way unsatisfactory – what would you have recommended?

CHAPTER *10*

The Practice of Preservation: Contexts

Every period has not only given us its own style of building … but also a restoration style of its own, with both successful and outrageous examples.
M H Van Swigchem, in *Monumentum*, Special Issue, 1975

This last chapter on philosophy in practice will concentrate on some broader conservation issues relating to the setting of buildings.

Living with the neighbours

A building that is robbed of the setting it was made for, is to that extent diminished. Whether the setting is raw nature, tamed nature, a designed ensemble or an informal grouping of buildings, and whether the loss occurs by deliberate destruction, unthinking erosion or the removal of the building to a completely different place, a relationship has been destroyed. Creating a new setting and a new relationship in such circumstances is one of the greatest tests a conservation architect or town planner can face. It is certainly a great deal easier to catalogue past failures than to celebrate the few notable successes.

Illustrations in earlier chapters have shown old buildings (or preserved bits of old buildings) reduced to meaningless relics by being attached to new developments of alien character. Alien here implies no judgement on the architectural quality of the new. It is simply a fact that in too many cases the new has barely acknowledged the presence of the old. Where there is neither common ancestry nor a real need for each other, the effect can be that of a steam whistle attached to a jumbo jet.

Contexts

Where development pressures are high, as in the City of London, unprotected buildings have little chance of survival. This can lead to irreversible damage to the historic character and the grain of the place, robbing the surviving preserved buildings of any sensible context.

10.1a Laurence Pountney, City of London. The late seventeenth-century houses in the right foreground were safely listed before the area came under pressure. The Victorian building in the background, which maintained the ancient line of the street and made a thoroughly pleasing job of turning the corner, was interesting in its own right, but had no protection.

10.1b The quality and townscape value of the unlisted building were appreciated too late. No action was taken to save it.

10.1c Its replacement paid no regard to the scale and character of the street. The old frontage lines were broken, creating a yawning gap where there had previously been an uninterrupted and visually satisfying architectural sequence. The seventeenth-century houses were not, in themselves, damaged but now look like isolated relics.

In a way, however, these are relatively small scale problems and, when it comes to weighing their appropriateness in conservation terms, they are also the least perplexing, since, in most cases, they should never have been allowed to happen at all. More interesting questions are raised and more subtle risks occur where it is the character of a whole place, rather than the setting of a single building that is at stake.

Examples of this kind of problem are numerous and readers will almost certainly be aware of particular cases that have not come to my notice. I shall draw particular attention to only two, both of which happen to involve famous domes.

10.2a The Cathedral of St Chad, Birmingham, (A W N Pugin 1839–56) has been crudely isolated by redevelopment and road works.

10.2b One of the road approaches to the Cathedral. Insult was added to injury by naming the pedestrian approach 'The Pugin Subway'.

10.3a A weatherboarded pub in Gravesend, North Kent provides a telling example of the reluctant preservation syndrome. A single glance shows it to be a clear candidate for preservation in any town centre redevelopment.

10.3b It has been preserved in the sense that it has not been demolished. In every other respect it has been totally ignored, an old offence made the more obvious by the care now being devoted to the regeneration of this town.

Since the mid-seventeenth century St Peter's in Rome has been approached through Bernini's Piazza San Pietro, a stupendous urban space surrounded by deep colonnades leading the eye to Maderno's west front. Michelangelo's great dome is set far back behind the nave, so that its full majesty can be appreciated only from the east or from a long distance. From the Piazza the upper part alone is visible and even an architect of Bernini's genius could make no more of it than a glimpsed promise of further architectural wonders to come. While the piazza was embedded in a dense weave of old streets, the relative insignificance of the dome was not a major disappointment. Standing or moving within this amazing, suddenly revealed space, there could be no sense of anticlimax.

When Mussolini's fascists came to power in Italy, in 1929, one of their first political acts was to conclude a treaty guaranteeing the status of the Vatican. To mark the occasion a celebratory highway was cut through the old city to connect St Peter's with the Castel Sant' Angelo. It certainly looked good on a map and the view it opened up was impressive from afar, but it destroyed the ancient urban texture and, by widening the entry, robbed the piazza of part of its impact. Moreover, as the basilica was approached from the new Via della Conciliazione, the dome appeared to sink slowly behind the west front, a decidedly anti-climactic effect.

The desire to open up views is, in some cases, a desire to be resisted. The removal of the relics of a dead riverside industry may provide the opportunity for the creation of a long riverside promenade, offering interesting and lively views of the industrial landscape on the opposite bank. If, however, that side eventually suffers the same fate (and why should one assume it will not?) the final effect may simply be dull and uninviting. The retention of some employable part of the old fabric, so that the path is sometimes on the waterfront itself, sometimes in narrow lanes between buildings or passing across old paved yards, will provide a far more interesting experience for the walker. The history of the place will also be more readily understood.

When Wren (and others) failed to impose a Renaissance plan on the City of London after the Great Fire, the new cathedral, raised on the site of the gothic St Paul's, had to be set into an irregular pattern of streets. The houses (and they were predominantly houses) were mostly rebuilt on their old frontage lines and to old property divisions, the one noticeable change being that the new buildings were predominantly of brick rather than timber. The cathedral must have appeared as an uncompromisingly modern giant, towering over them. The only other buildings rising noticeably above the rooftops were the church spires.

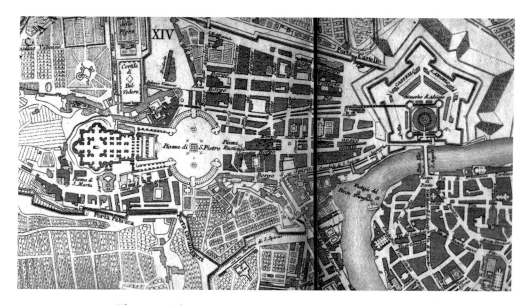

10.4 The twentieth-century opening up of a new view of St Peter's in Rome seemed a good idea at the time. This map of 1832 shows how Bernini, in the seventeenth century, had maintained the enclosure to his magnificent Piazza San Pietro.

More than 200 years later, the City (by this time, largely Victorian) suffered once more in the 1940–1 Blitz, and the area around Paternoster Row, between Newgate Street and St Paul's Churchyard, was totally obliterated. In the post-war years there was prolonged argument over the creation of a new setting for the cathedral until, in the 1950s, a plan by Lord Holford was adopted. This abandoned the old street pattern, substituting a grouping of slab blocks of various heights rising from decks approached by steps and intended to link with an ambitious system of upper level walkways penetrating every corner of the City. Building work was completed in 1967 but, thankfully, the City 'pedway' system, which would have made pedestrians safe by giving up the ground completely to traffic, never got beyond a few isolated fragments. It was eventually abandoned.

The Holford plan, much praised in its time, came under a great deal of criticism in later years as the architectural and planning orthodoxies of the 1950s and 60s were challenged. As a result (and aided by the surprising obsolescence – or lack of commercial appeal – of buildings still less than forty years old) the area has now (2003) once again undergone complete redevelopment.

There is a measure of historical inevitability about such swings of fortune. Whilst conservators may reasonably have views about the effect, for good or ill, of successive developments on the setting of the cathedral, they should be wary of joining in general choruses of fashionable approval or disapproval. Perhaps the important lesson for the conservation student to learn from all this is that the most carefully planned long term solutions can turn out to be astonishingly short-lived.

Set against a broader canvas, the dome of St Paul's has been a London ikon since it was built and its more distant views have excited a whole variety of protective actions over the years. One expression of this has been an insistence on the protection of 'the Canaletto view' from Westminster. This has always seemed to me to place the emphasis in the wrong place. Even if we had been unable to see the virtues of the long view until they were revealed to us by the camera obscura of a Venetian painter in the mid-eighteenth century – and I do not believe this was so – that particular view has been lost to us for a very long time.

What was of immense historic and environmental value was the skyline that Wren and his contemporaries gave to the post-fire City. It was a city with an instantly recognisable profile; a mighty dome surrounded by a prickle of spires of lively and varied shapes. This skyline survived recognisably until the 1930s and, with some sad war losses, through the 1950s. General roof levels had risen steadily in the passage of 250 years, but the

10.5a–c The London City skyline created by Wren and his contemporaries was eroded but not destroyed over the next two and a half centuries. Post-war reconstruction has changed it radically and permanently. The views shown date from 1820 (above), 1900 (opposite above), and 2002 (opposite below).

THE THAMES FROM WATERLOO BRIDGE: MENTIONED BY MR. WALTER CRANE AS AMONG THE MOST CHARACTERISTIC OF
From a Photo. by]   LONDON VIEWS.   [Geo. Newnes, Ltd.

effect was that of a slowly rising tide, reducing the impact of the individual spires but leaving the general pattern more or less intact. The arrival of the first office tower blocks changed all this. Planners, dedicated to the progress that the new forms represented, made valiant attempts to create corridors, free of tall buildings, to protect the distant views of the dome. In the immediate vicinity, the taller blocks were kept a decent distance from the cathedral itself, placed beyond the rim of a notional 'saucer'. But lacking a detailed knowledge of the modern historical background and viewing the resultant scene today, it would be difficult to deduce precisely what these measures were meant to achieve.

Once again it needs to be emphasised that it is neither the architectural qualities of the new buildings nor the honest intentions of the planning policies that are here in question, but rather the effectiveness of the action taken to protect what, by general consent, needed to be protected. The ideas looked good as words on paper but few, I think, would now claim that the modern City skyline and the dome's place within it is one of the great success stories of post-war planning. The Wren skyline (never mind 'the Canaletto view') has gone for ever. In both long and medium distance views the dome itself has become far less significant and in some views quite insignificant.

Living with the landscape

Maintaining the health and diversity of life on the planet is a vitally important conservation issue, but it is not one that can be dealt with adequately in a book whose whole focus is on historic buildings and built places. We cannot, however, completely ignore the fact that buildings exist in the natural world and that man's modifications of the natural world are sometimes so closely related to buildings that the two cannot be considered apart. Where historic buildings stand in the remnants of an historic landscape, there can be quite fierce arguments about what should be done.

The example of Greenwich Park is worth considering. The park is far from being a piece of surviving natural open space. Designed by Le Nôtre in the late seventeenth century, it was as much architecture as landscape, with chestnut avenues leading to the edge of a steep slope from which the visitor was given a suddenly revealed view of a Royal palace on the bank of the Thames. The effect is still striking, the more so by having Wren's Royal Observatory at the highest point, commanding the scene, with Inigo Jones's Queen's House and the old Royal Naval College below.

As originally conceived, the descent to the palace took the form of giant grassy steps or terraces. Through the eighteenth century this feature was eroded away until it became a long, slightly bumpy slope. The architectural effect was lost, but young couples visiting Greenwich Fair on high days and holidays would roll each other down what they called Roly Poly Hill, the unofficial name by which it is still best known. Today it is little children who roll down the hill, but until the fair was suppressed in 1856 it was adult males who most enjoyed the licence for mildly unseemly pleasure

10.6a Greenwich Park: Roly Poly Hill, the relic of a bold landscape design and, in its eroded condition, a place of childhood memories for many generations.

10.6b The view from Greenwich of the Queen's House, the Royal Naval College and the Isle of Dogs in 1968. The long axis of the chestnut avenue in Greenwich Park extended through the centre of this architectural composition to the distant spire of St Anne Limehouse.

10.6c The same view (now at the heart of a World Heritage Site) in 2002.

that fair days provided. The custom was to run down the hill hand in hand until the women fell and rolled, exposing legs and linen.

The restoration (or re-creation) of the terraces would complete a grand architectural landscape in a World Heritage site. It would, at the same time, extinguish a popular tradition that has lasted for around 250 years. My guess is that this landscape feature will eventually be restored, but it is difficult, in a case like this, to propose a course of action to please every-one. Adopting the careful conservator's habitual stance of doing nothing that does not actually need to be done would be regarded by some as unde-sirably continued neglect. Doing more could well be criticised by others as a kind of vandalism.

In Britain, perhaps more than in most other countries, a powerful national regard for trees can also lead to problems in maintaining or restoring historic landscapes. Designers of landscapes may not have lived to see their groves and avenues mature, but they would certainly have expected several following generations to enjoy what they had created. The time must always come, however, when the trees have grown to such a size that the intended effect is obscured. A careful programme of felling and replacement may be the best and only way to restore the designer's origi-nal intentions but, if started without open public consultation, it is almost certain to lead (probably should lead) to a 'save our fine old trees' cam-paign. We should never forget Baldwin Brown's 'force of intelligent belief'. No matter how carefully considered, well conceived and lawful our actions may be, if we lose the confidence of our public we can easily lose our authority to do anything at all.

On the crest of Shooter's Hill in south London is a memorial folly of 1784 in the form of a tall, triangular brick belvedere. It stood originally on the bare gravel hilltop, with expansive views over Kent. By the 1930s the views were still partly visible above treetops. Today the tower is almost completely enclosed by tall trees. It is no longer in any real sense a belvedere, a viewing tower, but it would be a very brave conservator indeed who proposed clearing the trees to expose the tower.

The compiling of a non-statutory register of park and gardens of spe-cial historic interest, which started in England in 1984, has already led to more systematic programmes of investigation of the non-built environ-ment. It can be confidently predicted that a parallel growth of public enthusiasm for (and understanding of) landscape conservation issues will follow. The obvious precedent for this is the great surge of public demand for the better care of the built environment which (as described in Chapter 4) became irresistible in the 1960s.

Death by design

Public concern for conservation in its widest sense, exerting pressure on even the least sensitive of planning authorities, has made the preserved amenity – the historic building desperately clinging on to life as an isolated relic in an alien setting – almost (but not quite) a thing of the unlamented past. A nearly opposite trend can, however, be almost as damaging, by clogging an historic building or place with a superfluity of contextual symbols.

This tendency is quite often observable when historic streets become pedestrianised, with wall-to-wall brick paving, cast iron bollards, gas pattern lamp standards and appropriate litter bins liberally sprinkled about. Individually the elements may be well designed and consonant with the character of the street, but the way they are disposed and their sheer concentration can produce an effect that has neither historical precedent nor practical inevitability to recommend it. Steering a satisfactory course between uncomfortable modern intrusions and what I have heard described as 'a nasty outbreak of heritage' can be tricky, but we must get better at it.

Considerable recent advances have been made (since 1967 in Britain) in the practice of conserving complete environments, but legislation and practice still seem to me to be seriously flawed (and this is a philosophical as well as a technical point) in failing to give sufficient detailed protection to ensembles of buildings. Our passion for grading can result in a row of, say, twenty buildings of varied individual quality in a conservation area having half a dozen statutorily protected elements (in three grades), a further half-dozen included in a local list with no statutory force, and eight with no recognition whatever beyond their inclusion in the designated area.

If the whole ensemble has a value that is greater than the sum of its parts and if every element makes some contribution to its special quality, should it not be protected as if it were one building? All too often we see a group which has reached its present pleasing form by a process of accretion and replacement and which might well stand some further slow instalments of change, forced to suffer massive renewal over a very short period – all in the name of conservation. An interesting sequence of individuals of different ages and degrees of ambition, perpetuating old development patterns, can by this process be turned into a self-consciously created setting for a few handsome antiques whose presence merely advertises the offence that has been committed. The devices employed to echo the visual intricacy of the original group and the styles adopted for the new buildings (traditional, frankly modern or reticent to the point of total anonymity) are, in such a context, of marginal relevance. This kind of large-scale renewal may, on occasions, be the least bad way of reinvigorating an area near to death, but the obliteration of the history of the place is final. It cannot actually be made good by clever design.

All concerned in any way with building conservation should be concerned to prevent this kind of damage. We do not protect only the ornamental parts of a listed building and dismiss the rest as unimportant connecting fabric which could be replaced by something new and appropriate (see Chapter 9, 'Degrees of violence', for a consideration of the tell-me-which-bits-are-listed fallacy). So why do we do it with pieces of the town?

CHAPTER *11*

Final Thoughts

Reconstruction, resiting, resurrection and anastylosis

At various points in this study we have considered how different times and different agencies have dealt with historic buildings with widely varying degrees of violence and tenderness. We now need to examine several related kinds of intervention which, at first sight, seem too radical to be regarded as acceptable conservation procedures but which are, nevertheless, undertaken at times by perfectly respectable practitioners.

In Chapter 9 the insidiously attractive arguments surrounding façadism and other kinds of skin-deep preservation were examined. It was shown that pursuing these arguments to their logical conclusion could make every erosive act a justification for the next, leading ultimately to total or near-total renewal. By this process, a supposedly preserved building may become no more than a dim image of itself, reducing eloquent messages from the past to a sort of telegraphic gobbledegook.

Leaving aside exceptional, emotionally charged, cases (like the re-creation of old Warsaw quoted in that chapter) there can surely be few circumstances where really large scale reconstruction or re-creation is justifiable in conservation terms, even when there is the most faithful reproduction of material and detail, inside and out. Nevertheless, as we have seen repeatedly in this study, it is difficult to state any rule so hard that it does not have, somewhere, a soft edge. We have already noted, as something of a curiosity, an example of a theatre interior re-created after a lapse of time within a modern building (page 100). More to the point, some North American practitioners would argue that a meticulously researched resurrection of a building whose site is now identifiable by only a few fragments may be permissible if that building is vitally important to an understanding of the history of the nation or the place.

Colonial Williamsburg, where not only the built fabric but the daily life of a small pre-Revolutionary town have been revealed and re-created is too extraordinary a case to be regarded as a precedent, desirable or otherwise, in conservation terms. It is essentially a very special and successful kind of museum. But museums of buildings, like those at Singleton in Sussex and St Fagans near Cardiff, do raise issues of immediate relevance to the conservator. These places are rescue homes of last resort.

We considered in the last chapter the questions posed by buildings that have lost their original surroundings. We should note next the related but less common case of the building that has itself been removed from its original context, its local associations and its historical (and perhaps archaeologically significant) site. It too must, to that extent, be regarded as damaged. Nevertheless, if its circumstances leave no prospect of preservation *in situ*, a faithful reconstruction in a place where it can be appreciated and effectively interpreted in a congruous setting may reasonably be preferred to total loss. Before adopting such a radical course of action, however, we must be satisfied that there is absolutely no alternative to removal and that the receiving agency has the financial means, the scholarship and the craft skills to deal with the building in a proper manner.

Some forms of construction, for example timber or iron frames, are more amenable to this kind of 'last ditch' preservation than masonry or earth buildings, but the resiting, of a whole variety of structures has been practised for a very long time and with no motive beyond that of improving utility. The method adopted for buildings of manageable size, especially in North America, has not uncommonly been corseting, lifting and transportation, without dismantling. With modern technology and where no great distances are involved, this can be an economical procedure, but when historic buildings are treated in this way (and it usually done to clear the ground for some completely unrelated project) the results can be ludicrous.

A timber-framed fifteenth/sixteenth-century group, formerly standing in Manchester's Old Shambles and including an inn scheduled as an ancient monument, was moved bodily and placed at a 30 ft higher level within a massive new town centre development. The confusion of ideas at work in this reverential attack on history is difficult to unpick, but it was celebrated at the time as an engineering feat (which it certainly was) and a great conservation achievement (which it was not). It may have been a well-intentioned action, but I suspect this spectacular resiting was really no more than a symbol of preservation in an ocean of destruction. The group is now a lonely curiosity, lacking all historical context. It does not even stand on the ground. It is hard to believe that, in the process of redesigning a whole city centre, there was no will to find a solution that would leave the last timber-framed buildings in central Manchester *in situ*, to form an interesting link between the ancient and modern topography of the city.

In the City of London in 1954 a Roman Mithraic temple was discovered during excavation for the lower storeys of a new building. The discovery of this rich site came at a distressingly late moment. There was at that time no mandatory requirement for site investigation before building but the contract was, in the event, delayed long enough for the remains to be investigated and recorded and for important artefacts to be recovered. The temple was finally raised, not bodily in this case but piece by piece to ground level. Here it was put back together on a new site where it can still be seen. It is now no longer on or even immediately above its original position, its alignment has been turned through 90° and stone has replaced the timber elements in its original construction. As a monument of Roman London it is deeply compromised, but the temper of the time would have allowed no better result. As a record of ambivalent attitudes to the past in the 1950s, the Temple of Mithras could hardly be bettered.

11.1 The Temple of Mithras, excavated in 1954, was reconstructed at modern ground level and at some distance from its original site. An outstandingly important discovery, its preservation in this form is regarded today as only marginally better than destruction and far less desirable than re-burying *in situ* (which was not, however, an available option at the time). Present procedures of site investigation prior to redevelopment are generally effective in avoiding the need for this kind of panic treatment.

What, then, are we to think of the dismantling and re-erection of the temples and monuments of Abu Simbel to escape inundation after the building of the high dam at Aswan? Here there was no late discovery, no confusion of ideas and no question as to what was at stake. But neither was there any prospect of a design solution, short of abandoning the dam project, which was itself a potent symbol of national pride. Objects of world importance, whose immense artistic and archaeological significance was beyond argument, were going to disappear. The only choice was between doing nothing or moving the gigantic monuments to a higher level. Agonising decisions had to be taken but, in this case, the solution had to be to adopt the least undesirable course. The monuments can still be seen in all their majesty. But no solution is ever perfect. Wind erosion has proved to be a problem on the new site.

The total re-erection and/or resiting of monuments are not everyday problems. But in the world of archaeology, the question of partial reconstruction arises with regularity.

All reconstructive work [to ruins] should be ruled out a priori. Only anastylosis, that is to say, the reassembling of existing but dismembered parts can be permitted. The material used for integration should always be recognisable and its use should be the least that will ensure the conservation of a monument and the reinstatement of its form.
Venice Charter, 1964

It is often difficult to decide whether anastylosis is justified. Meaningless heaps of stones do not give an instructive message to the beholder... Anastylosis is full of pitfalls, as the re-erection of fallen stones is never certain to be correct. Many examples can be quoted, but one of the earliest is Sir Arthur Evans's attempt to make Knossos more intelligible by re-erecting parts of the palace. Archaeologists now say he was wrong, but boatloads of cultural tourists to Crete have been grateful to him for the attempt, which helps them interpret and understand the site.
Sir Bernard Feilden *Conservation of Historic Buildings*, Ch. 17, 1994 edition

Many visitors to archaeological sites and preserved ruins are unable to read the remains effectively (which in this context also means pleasurably) even with the help of diagrams and interpretive displays. The judicious re-erection of fallen masonry can add materially to understanding and may also, on occasions, be justified as structurally prudent, to prevent further deterioration or to make good historically recent misadventures. In 1958–9 one of the trilithons and a single bay of the lintelled ring at Stonehenge were restored after recorded falls of masonry in 1797 and 1900. In both cases, views existed of the monument before damage and the work was firmly based on exhaustive investigation. As the distinguished archaeologist, M W Thompson observed, 'the improvement in the intelligibility of the plan caused by the re-erection is profound'.

The Stonehenge restorations were made entirely with original elements, still lying on the site, but occasions frequently arise where new material is needed to make good lacunae. It may be necessary, for example, to replace an absent or dangerously decayed mullion where a lintel or an otherwise complete traceried window is in danger of collapse. Again, the re-erection of a column from its recovered parts may call for new material, where one or more of the parts is missing or badly damaged. In these circumstances the *Venice Charter* insists that the new work 'should always be recognisable'. This is obviously necessary if authenticity is to be maintained without deliberate deception, but the requirement may be observed in more ways than one.

The choices are really not very different from those discussed in Chapter 8 in relation to the restoration of frescos and in Chapter 9 under the heading 'Visible or invisible?' The use of brick as connecting fabric for stone or marble is about as honest as one can get in distinguishing new from old (much work of this kind can be seen in, for example, the Forum in Rome) but has the disadvantage of being visible a quarter of a mile away. One possible alternative is to use similar but discernibly different new material or to use matching material which is given surface treatment to distinguish it from the original elements (rather in the way that some art restorers use striae). The effect can be aesthetically pleasing, but the nearer the match, the more necessary it will be to avert possible confusion by, for example, a discreet date inscription on the new work.

Public opinion and fashion

Fashion is a poor guide to what should be preserved. If fashionable taste had prevailed, 'monstrosities' (the word is an infallible signal that a type of building currently unadmired is about to be mentioned) like St Pancras Station Hotel would have been demolished without a murmur in the 1950s and practically every plain Georgian terrace would have been sacrificed at any time before World War II. Some fine buildings have had the good fortune to survive the metamorphosis from 'monstrosity' to 'masterpiece' (an equally overworked word, commonly misused to denote fashionable approval) but many have been lost because their real qualities were obscured by prejudice. What they were said to be was more important – for the time being – than what they actually were.

Current popular taste is also a shaky guide to how, as well as whether, particular buildings should be preserved – especially when the taste is that of a possibly short-term commercial occupant.

11.2a Public opinion is rightly powerful in determining how effectively the provisions for building preservation can work. Passing fashion, however, is an ill-informed and fickle guide to special interest and quality. It is no guide at all to the manner in which buildings should be preserved. If fashionable opinion had determined its fate, the Midland Hotel at St Pancras (Sir George Gilbert Scott 1874) would have been destroyed at any time between the 1930s and 1960s. It is now listed as Grade I, a status which is generally accepted as being appropriate to one of the great architectural inventions of the nineteenth century.

11.2b By contrast, the St Pancras train shed has, for most of its life, been recognised as a great work of engineering genius (W H Barlow and R M Ordish).

But how does all this square with Baldwin Brown's insistence that public opinion provides the only authority for preservation of historic buildings?

He was, of course, right. Authority for interference with the rights of private owners can only be based on what he called 'a force of intelligent belief in the mind of the people'. The strength of public opinion will thus determine the 'bite' of the protective legislation but the ways in which buildings are preserved must be left to those specially skilled. To take a fairly obvious parallel: public opinion determined that there should be a National Health Service. It is, nevertheless, doctors not voters who make diagnoses and prescribe treatments.

Public opinion, as Baldwin Brown remarked, tends to act spasmodically upon the stimulus supplied by some striking event. Trends of taste or opinion may make it easier or more difficult to preserve certain kinds of building, devote public funds to their support, put them to the uses most conducive to their survival and carry out works in a satisfactory manner. Such trends cannot, however, alter the facts.

Conservation specialists have to work within current constraints but they must themselves be concerned with facts, not fashions. Their responsibility is to future generations as well as to the present. It follows that they have a duty, whether as advisers to individual clients or as officials serving a community, to be effective advocates for all the buildings, loved or unloved, which pass through their hands.

11.3 The Folies Bergere, Paris (1872 and 1888, altered by Piolenc et Morice 1928) belongs to a class of buildings for long unnoticed by the public and disregarded by architectural historians. The 1928 facade is now seen as a remarkable work of its kind and date. It finally obtained statutory protection in the 1990s, but the main fabric of the Folies, although recognised as being of some interest, still lacks full protection.

11.4 Strand, London. Swings of opinion can leave ugly scars. Epstein's nude figures on the British Medical Association building excited furious controversy when they were first seen. The *Evening Standard* in June 1908 declared that they constituted 'a form of statuary which no careful father would wish his daughter or no discerning young man his fiancée to see'. By 1938, with the building in different occupation, reaction had expressed itself violently. Looking at the severely defaced, but still impressive, figures today it is difficult to believe that anyone could have taken a club hammer to them.

A true record

A well-preserved building should speak with a clear voice, presenting a true record of itself, but a building is a complex organism which cannot at one glance reveal every relevant fact about its physical nature and past history. The effects of past interventions encountered during repair works can be mystifying and even lead to dangerously wrong diagnoses if misread. It should be recognised as a duty by anyone entrusted with any aspect of works to an historic building, not only to record meticulously what has been done on this occasion (which may not be quite the same thing as what was initially intended) but also what new facts have been discovered in the course of the work.

For the sake of one's professional successors, as well as in the interests of history, the record of the building as found and the description of the work done should be as full and accurate as they can be made, using whatever techniques or combination of techniques – measured drawing, sketches, site notes, photography, photogrammetry, annotated contract documents, etc – are appropriate.

No record, however slight, which may conceivably be of some use in the future, should be discarded or destroyed.

CHAPTER *12*

Conclusion

Monuments are greatly subject to wear and tear … The question is whether continuous partial restoration does not lead in the long run to the same result as reconstruction after the original model, to wit: building of a full-scale replica … There is a limit to what a building can take.
M H Van Swigchem, in *Monumentum*, Special Issue, 1975

The Japanese temple complex of Ise Naiku in Honshu Province has been replicated every twenty years since the reign of Emperor Temmu (673–686)… In the humid climate of Japan, untreated timbers sawn of [pale yellow cypress] have a very short life. Immortality could be won only by periodic replication.
James Marston Fitch, *Historic Preservation*, 1990 edition

…Put protection in place of restoration… stave off decay by daily care… prop a perilous wall or mend a leaky roof… and otherwise resist all tampering with either the fabric or the ornament of the building as it stands…
Society for the Protection of Ancient Buildings, *Manifesto* 1877

I head the final chapter 'conclusion', meaning simply 'end', rather than 'conclusions' because the latter suggests a summary which may be dashed through by someone too hurried to take in the whole text. This conclusion will be a disappointment to such a reader.

One devastating thought has been kept to the very end. All the philosophical attitudes and policy statements examined in this paper amount, in the end, to a monocular view of what conservation is about. We have looked with only one eye – the Western one.

Modern Monuments

The word monument falls strangely in relation to works many of whose creators would have been thoroughly discomfited at the very idea of their buildings being so regarded. Nevertheless, from the viewpoint of this study, the philosophical issues surrounding the care of modern buildings need to be considered.

12.1 The Paris (Beaubourg) Pompidou Centre (Piano and Rogers 1977) might be seen by some as a celebratory monument of the same order, albeit very different kind, as the Garnier Opera (see 4.1b) but its maintenance present quite different problems from those of a masonry building. Where the technical works are such a visible and essential part of the architectural conception, new philosophical questions arise. For example, what should happen in, say, 30 or 40 years time when the many pieces of technical apparatus, even complete systems, are completely overtaken and may not be replaceable, like for like? Should the replacements adopt some sort of disguise to resemble the old – an approach which might well be dismissed as absurd in relation to such a revolutionary building of its time? Or should the building simply be allowed to change, accommodating the new technology in whatever form is practically acceptable? Such issues may not arise for some long time, but when they do, there are likely to be powerful conflicts of opinion. And recent experience has shown that architects with little overt interest in conservation as such can be extremely sensitive about the fate of their own works. Alan Powers' essay on 'What are we trying to conserve?' (in *Preserving Post War Heritage*, 2001; see Bibliography) is relevant to this argument.

12.2a and 12.2b An early example of a modern movement building in Britain is a house, originally concrete-faced, by Gropius and Fry in Chelsea Old Church Street (above). The blackened artificial slate hanging dealt with a severe maintenance problem, but no amount of skill in execution of this solution can make up for the loss of the original geometrical purity of design, still crisply visible in its neighbour (by Mendelsohn and Chermayeff, 1936) (below).

In most oriental cultures the idea of going through agonies of con-science over the preservation of particular morsels of old fabric simply because they are old would not be seen as entirely reasonable. From this alternative viewpoint, a building has an indestructible soul; a permanent reality, which can survive any amount of renewal including, in the case of the most ancient and revered monuments, a succession of total rebuilds from the ground up.

Before dismissing this behaviour as too alien to be relevant to our Western sensibilities and experience, consider the implications of our own determined attempts to make buildings last for ever. We have already looked at the ways in which ordinary, judicious repair inevitably leads to the introduction of new material (Chapter 9, under 'Repair and replacement'). However surgical and cunning our techniques and however reluctant our interventions, there is no escaping the fact that continuous care mean pro-gressive, even repeated renewal (or accepted loss) of original fabric. At the very least it can lead to the concealment of original finishes by, for example, periodic repainting. Some programmes (for example, those applied to the British Royal Palaces for well over a century) have aimed at so high a stan-dard of care as to cause committed SPAB-conditioned conservators to wonder whether they are looking at historical reality or reincarnation.

A respected conservation expert has suggested that some key International Modern buildings are, by reason of their vulnerable materi-als and construction, now so difficult to conserve effectively that it might be more sensible to reconstruct them faithfully to the original designs, modified only to achieve longer life. The very idea (and see again Chapter 9 on 'Restoration and reproduction') can promote furious argument amongst those conditioned to a Western understanding of conservation.

The fact that we find the question worth discussing marks the essential difference between two equally valid world views of conservation and underlines the fact that what we do is conditioned by our motives in doing anything at all.

The thought I wish to leave you with is the one I started with – that a sound philosophy is not based on a set of immutables rules but on a clear understanding of what, in each instance, conservation is setting out to achieve. Comprehensive knowledge of all the relevant facts (the impor-tance of which has been emphasised throughout) will not, of itself, point the way. The practitioner, and this applies not only to those in direct con-trol of works, must develop a critical and self-critical frame of mind, nur-turing the ability to proceed from facts by way of logical argument to defensible – if not inevitable – conclusions.

12.3 The two most striking secular buildings in Morecambe are the Victoria Pavilion of 1896 and the Midland Hotel (Oliver Hill) (right) of 1936, both of which owe their existence to the town's former status as a great coastal resort. With the decline of the British seaside holiday, the future of both buildings has been in serious doubt but this has made their preservation all the more important. The Midland Hotel, in particular, is such a prominent object on the seafront that its condition will always be a highly visible barometer of the condition and morale of the town itself.

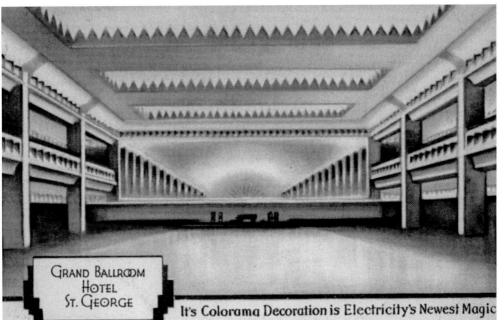

GRAND BALLROOM
HOTEL
ST. GEORGE

It's Colorama Decoration is Electricity's Newest Magic

12.4 An American ballroom with 'Colorama' decorative lighting. Some mid-twentieth-century buildings, particularly in the entertainment field, used washes of coloured light, as much as three-dimensional modelling to achieve their aesthetic effect. Such buildings can be quite sad objects when robbed of their 'architecture of light' but, well restored, even relatively modest examples may provide vivid illustrations of 1930s taste and leisure.

No text of this kind can hope to do more than exercise the mind in readiness for the practical tests of daily professional life. You should now look at the work of the best practitioners and study their philosophies (they very often attach 'my' to the word 'philosophy'); but don't stop there. You should also cast a questioning eye over everything you see done in the name of conservation, from the least demanding 'lick and a promise' to the most unsympathetic commercial blastaway refurbishment. Philosophical insights are to be gained from a consideration of the humdrum and the frankly awful as well as the exemplary.

Finally, whatever your personal role in the conservation processes, remember that, for the time being, the building, the ensemble, the street or the town is under your protection. It is a heavy responsibility and one that had better be faced philosophically.

Chronology (from 1800)

This chronology identifies some milestones in the history of attitudes to conservation and the development of protective laws. It is not intended to be comprehensive and, in particular, it makes no attempt to include every recent British government direction or circular.

Fully italicised entries concern Great Britain

1801/2 Carlo Fea appointed Commissioner of Antiquities and Antonio Canova appointed Inspector of Fine Arts for the Papal States. Doria Pamphili Edict of 1802 concerned mainly with works of art and 'finds' but recalling earlier Papal edicts and prohibiting injury to ancient monuments and ruined structures.

1807 Danish Royal Commission for the conservation of antiquities established.

1815 Schinkel's report to Prussian government on relics of mediaeval art damaged in French wars.

1818 Grand Duchy of Hesse introduces laws to inventorise and protect monuments. Other Prussian states take similar action about this time.

1830 France appoints General Inspector of Ancient Monuments.

1834 First Greek monuments legislation (reformed and extended 1899).

1835 Bavaria appoints full-time conservators of monuments.

1837 France sets up Commission for Historical Monuments and begins inventorisation and major works of repair and restoration. Viollet-le-Duc appointed.

1852 French Commission introduces measure to protect great vistas and monumental perspectives.

1853 Prussian monuments commission appointed (ineffective due to lack of funds).

1865 *Commons Preservation Society formed.*

1872 Attempt to consolidate provincial monuments measures in Italy fails.

1872 *Ecclesiastical Architects and Surveyors Association formed (as 'Surveyors of Ecclesiastical Dilapidations').*

1873 *First British Ancient Monuments Bill fails.*

1874 *Society for Photographing Relics of Old London begins work, reflecting growing awareness of rate of loss of old buildings.*

1877 *William Morris's letter to the Athenaeum. Society for the Protection of Ancient Buildings (SPAB) founded. The Society's* Manifesto *published (see Appendix 2).*

1882 *First British Ancient Monuments Act. Only 68 monuments included in schedule. Provision for taking scheduled monuments into public ownership by agreement, but no compulsory powers affecting owners.*

1887–9 French Historical Monuments 'Law of 30 March 1887' (published with inventory 1889) confirms expropriation powers and confers extensive powers over 2200 'monuments classés' (later extended and reinforced).

1893 *London County Council acquires the York Water Gate as an object of interest that is in danger of falling into decay.*

1894 *Committee for the Survey of the Memorials of Greater London formed (C R Ashbee, Chairman) (first published monograph 1896).*

1895 *National Trust for Places of Historic Interest and Natural Beauty formed. Incorporated by Act of Parliament in 1907 and now has extensive land holdings in England, Wales and N Ireland (National Trust for Scotland 1931).*

1897 *London County Council hosts conference on listing of London's historic buildings.*

1898 *London County Council obtains general power to acquire and preserve historic buildings.*

1900 *Ancient Monuments Protection Act, extends protective provisions of 1882 Act; County Councils given powers to preserve and maintain monuments.*

1900 *First parish volume of Survey of London.*

1901 *First volume of VCH published (Victoria History of the Counties of England).*

1902   Monuments legislation for whole of Italy (extended 1909 and later).

1905   *Gerard Baldwin Brown's* Care of Ancient Monuments *published.*

1908   *Royal Commissions on Historical Monuments appointed for England, Wales and Scotland (concerned with inventorisation and recording).*

1913   *Ancient Monuments Consolidation and Amendment Act; provision made for listing of monuments and making of preservation orders (later amended and reinforced by Ancient Monuments Act 1931, Historic Buildings and Ancient Monuments Act 1953, and Field Monuments Act 1972).*

1921   *Council for Places of Worship (Council for the Care of Churches) founded.*

1924   *Ancient Monuments Society founded.*

1924   *Royal Fine Art Commission founded.*

1926   *Council for the Protection of Rural England(CPRE) founded (CPR Wales in 1928).*

1931   *Athens Charter* adopted at the First International Congress of Architects and Technicians of Historic Monuments (see 1964).

1932   *Town and Country Planning Act introduces 'building preservation orders'. Local authorities given power to make such orders to protect buildings of special architectural or historic interest, but no provision made for inventorisation.*

1932   Vieux Carré Commission (New Orleans La USA) law to preserve buildings and character of the French Quarter.

1937   *Georgian Group founded.*

1941   *National Buildings (later Monuments) Record founded.*

1944–7   *Town and Country Planning Acts require Minister to compile statutory lists of buildings of special architectural or historic interest; two months notice required of demolition or alteration; building preservation order provisions re-enacted.*

1946   *Instructions to Investigators for the Listing of Buildings … issued.*

1950   *Gower Report on Country Houses.*

1951   *First volume of Pevsner's* Buildings of England *published.*

1953   *Historic Buildings and Ancient Monuments Act (see 1913); Historic Buildings Council for England founded (1983 absorbed into English Heritage).*

1957   *Civic Trust founded.*

1957   International Congress of Architects and Specialists of Historic Buildings in Paris. See second meeting in 1964 in Venice.

1957   *Friends of Friendless Churches founded.*

1958   *Victorian Society founded.*

1962   *Local Authorities (Historic Buildings) Act confers powers to make grants or loans to owners to repair historic buildings.*

1962   French *Loi Malraux* for the definition, protection and restoration of historic areas.

1964   *Venice Charter* (International Charter for the Conservation of Monuments and Sites) adopted by the newly formed International Council on Monuments and Sites (ICOMOS) at the Second International Congress of Architects and Technicians. Building on the Athens Charter (1931) and the Paris Congress (1957), the Charter was published by ICOMOS in 1966.

1967   *Civic Amenities Act introduces concept of conservation areas.*

1968   *Town and Country Planning Act abolishes notice system and abolishes building preservation orders. Introduces listed building consent procedure. Introduces repairs notices, building preservation notices and further strengthens protective laws. Crown buildings no longer excluded from listing.*

1968   UNESCO *Recommendations* concerning preservation of cultural property endangered by public or private works.

1968   *Association for Studies in the Conservation of Historic Buildings founded.*

1968   Association for Preservation Technology formally constituted in North America.

1968   *Pastoral Measure, concerned mainly with Church of England church redundancy procedures (and see later 1983).*

1969   *Redundant Churches and Other Religious Buildings Act; Redundant Churches Fund established.*

1969   European convention on the protection of the Archaeological Heritage adopted by the Council of Europe.

1969   *Committee for Environmental Conservation founded.*

1969   *Comprehensive review of statutory lists commenced.*

1971   *Town and Country Planning Act (consolidating measure).*

1972   *Town and Country Planning (Amendment) Act; funds to be provided for conservation schemes.*

1972   Convention for the Protection of World Cultural and Natural Heritage (*World Heritage Convention*) adopted by UNESCO. Introduces the concept of World Heritage sites.

1972 *Field Monuments Act.*

1974 *Town and Country Amenities Act strengthening demolition controls in conservation areas.*

1975 *SAVE Britain's Heritage founded.*

1975 European Charter of the Architectural Heritage (*Declaration of Amsterdam*) adopted by Council of Europe. European Architectural Heritage Year declared.

1975 *Final Report of RIBA/COTAC Joint Study Group recommending objectives, form and content for a course in architectural building conservation.*

1976 *Theatres Trust Act.*

1976 UNESCO *Recommendations* concerning the safeguarding and contemporary role of historic areas.

1976 Charter of Cultural Tourism (*Brussels Charter*) adopted by ICOMOS.

1976 US Secretary of the Interior's *Standards for Rehabilitation ...* for Historic Buildings published (later revised, see 1984).

1979 *Ancient Monuments and Archaeological Areas Act introduces consent system for archaeological sites, similar to listed building consent; also introduces 'archaeological areas' where developers must allow access for archaeological investigation.*

1979 Australian charter for the conservation of places of cultural significance (*Burra Charter*) adopted by Australia ICOMOS (amended extended in 1981, 1988 and 1999).

1979 *Thirties Society founded (later named Twentieth Century Society).*

1980 *National Heritage Memorial Act.*

1981 *Association of Conservation Officers founded (see 1997).*

1982 *Florence Charter* on Historic Gardens adopted by ICOMOS.

1982 Charter for the Preservation of Quebec's Heritage (*Declaration of Deschambault*) adopted by the Conseil des monuments et des sites du Quebec, ICOMOS Canada French-speaking Committee.

1983 *Pastoral Measure (see 1968).*

1983 *Appleton Charter* for the Protection and Enhancement of the Built Environment adopted by ICOMOS Canada English-speaking Committee.

1983 *National Heritage Act establishes Historic Buildings and Monuments Commission for England ('English Heritage') and Historic Scotland.*

1984   US Secretary of the *Interior's Standards for Rehabilitation and Guidelines for Rehabilitating Historic Buildings* revised and published by US Dept of the Interior, National Park Service, Preservation Assistance Division (see 1976).

1984   *World Heritage Convention ratified by UK.*

1985   Canadian *Code of Ethics* and guidance for practice for those involved in the conservation of cultural property in Canada published by International Institute for Conservation, Conservators' Group, Ottawa (see Appendix 5).

1985   Convention for the Protection of the Architectural Heritage of Europe (*Granada Convention*) adopted by the Council of Europe.

1987   Charter for the Conservation of *Historic Towns and Urban Areas* adopted by ICOMOS.

1987   First Brazilian Seminar on preservation and revitalization of historic centres; *Carta de Petropolis* published by ICOMOS Brazil committee.

1987   *Circular 8/87 issued; a major statement of government conservation policies. '30 year rule' introduced enabling buildings over 30 years old to be considered for listing (see 1994 PPG 15).*

1988   *First Register of Parks and Gardens of Special Historic Interest in England completed. See 1995.*

1990   International Charter for *Archaeological Heritage Management* adopted by ICOMOS.

1990   *Inauguration of RICS Diploma Course in Building Conservation.*

1990   *Town and Country Planning Act, together with Planning (Listed Buildings and Conservation Areas) Act 1990, became the principal Acts, consolidating and re-enacting the provisions of the 1971 Act (as amended). Ancient Monuments legislation (see 1979) not affected.*

1990   *Planning Policy Guidance Note on Archaeology and Planning (PPG 16) issued.*

1991   *Repair of Historic Buildings: Advice on Principles and Methods, published by English Heritage.*

1992   *Department of National Heritage created with a broad arts and heritage brief and inheriting from Department of the Environment extensive powers in relation to historic buildings.*

1993   *National Lottery Act leads to creation of a new source of 'heritage' funding.*

1993   *Code of Practice on the Care of Churches and Ecclesiastical Jurisdiction Measure (General Synod of Church of England).*

1993   ICOMOS *Guidelines for Education and Training* in the conservation of monuments, ensembles and sites.

1994   *Planning Policy Guidance Note on Planning and the Historic Environment (PPG 15) issued, superseding Circular 8/87 as a statement on government policies.*

1995   *Planning authorities required to consult English Heritage and Garden History Society on applications for development affecting registered gardens (see 1988). Upgrading of the register commenced the following year.*

1997   *Department of Culture, Media and Sport created; takes over built heritage brief as successor to Department of National Heritage (see 1992).*

1997   *Institute of Historic Buildings Conservation (IHBC) formed by former Association of Conservation Officers (see 1981).*

1998   *British Standard Guide to Principles of Conservation of Historic Buildings published (BS 7913).*

1999   *Burra Charter (see 1979) revised and republished by Australia ICOMOS.*

2001–2   *Planning and conservation laws and procedures undergoing extensive review.*

APPENDIX 2

The SPAB Manifesto

Much has been made of the 1877 *Manifesto* in this study and it may surprise the reader to find how much of it consists of anti-restoration polemic and how little (essentially the last two paragraphs) with commending a philosophy of care. It was, nevertheless, this brief statement which fixed the starting line for most modern philosophical analyses.

Society for the Protection of Ancient Buildings

MANIFESTO

A Society coming before the public with such a name as that above written must needs explain how, and why, it proposes to protect those ancient buildings which, to most people doubtless, seem to have so many and such excellent protectors. This, then, is the explanation we offer.

No doubt within the last fifty years a new interest, almost like another sense, has arisen in these ancient monuments of art; and they have become the subject of one of the most interesting of studies, and of an enthusiasm, religious, historical, artistic, which is one of the undoubted gains of our time; yet we think that if the present treatment of them be continued, our descendants will find them useless for study and chilling to enthusiasm. We think that those last fifty years of knowledge and attention have done more for their destruction than all the foregoing centuries of revolution, violence, and contempt.

For Architecture, long decaying, died out, as a popular art at least, just as the knowledge of mediaeval art was born. So that the civilised world of the nineteenth century has no style of its own amidst its wide knowledge of the styles of other centuries. From this lack and this gain arose in men's minds the strange idea of the Restoration of ancient buildings; and a strange and most fatal idea, which by its very name implies that it is possible to strip from a building this, that, and the other part of its history – of its life that is – and then to stay the hand at some arbitrary point, and leave it still historical, living, and even as it once was.

In early times this kind of forgery was impossible, because knowledge failed the builders, or perhaps because instinct held them back. If repairs were needed, if ambition or piety pricked on to change, that change was of necessity wrought in the unmistakable fashion of the time; a church of the eleventh century might be added to or altered in the twelfth, thirteenth, fourteenth, fifteenth, sixteenth, or even the seventeenth or eighteenth centuries; but every change, whatever history it destroyed, left history in the gap, and was alive with the spirit of the deeds done midst its fashioning. The result of all this was often a building in which the many changes, though harsh and visible enough, were, by their very contrast, interesting and instructive and could by no possibility mislead. But those who make the changes wrought in our day under the name of Restoration, while professing to bring back a building to the best time of its history, have no guide but each his own individual whim to point out to them what is admirable and what contemptible; while the very nature of their tasks compels them to destroy something and to supply the gap by imagining what the earlier builders should or might have done. Moreover, in the course of this double process of destruction and addition the whole surface of the building is necessarily tampered with; so that the appearance of antiquity is taken away from such old parts of the fabric as are left, and there is no laying to rest in the spectator the suspicion of what may have been lost; and in short, a feeble and lifeless forgery is the final result of all the wasted labour.

It is sad to say, that in this manner most of the bigger Minsters, and a vast number of more humble buildings, both in England and on the Continent, have been dealt with by men of talent often, and worthy of better employment, but deaf to the claims of poetry and history in the highest sense of the words.

For what is left we plead before our architects themselves, before the official guardians or buildings, and before the public generally, and we pray them to remember how much is gone of the religion, thought and manners of time past, never by almost universal consent, to be Restored; and to consider whether it be possible to Restore those buildings, the living spirit of which, it cannot be too often repeated, was an inseparable part of that religion and thought, and those past manners. For our part we assure them fearlessly, that of all the Restorations yet undertaken the worst have meant the reckless stripping a building of some of its most interesting material features; whilst the best have their exact analogy in the Restoration of an old picture, where the partly-perished work of the ancient craftsmaster has been made neat and smooth by the tricky hand of some unoriginal and thoughtless hack of today. If, for the rest, it be asked us to specify what kind of amount of art, style, or other interest in a building, makes it worth protecting, we answer, anything which can be looked on as artistic, picturesque, historical, antique, or substantial: any work, in short, over which educated, artistic people would think it worth while to argue at all.

It is for all these buildings, therefore, of all times and styles, that we plead, and call upon those who have to deal with them to put Protection in the place of Restoration, to stave off decay by daily care, to prop a perilous wall or mend a leaky roof by such means as are obviously meant for support or covering, and show no pretence of other art, and otherwise to resist all tampering with either the fabric or ornament of the building as it stands; if it has become inconvenient for its present use, to raise another building rather than alter or enlarge the old one; in fine to treat our ancient buildings as monuments of a bygone art, created by bygone manners, that modern art cannot meddle with without destroying.

Thus, and thus only, shall we escape the reproach of our learning being turned into a snare to us; thus, and thus only can we protect our ancient buildings, and hand them down instructive and venerable to those that come after us.

Commentary

Here in the *Manifesto*, three basic tenets, which had emerged in decades of controversy and which were to influence all subsequent debate, were stated concisely for the first time.

1. We are custodians of the ancient buildings we have inherited. We should not regard ourselves as free to do as we please with them.
2. Effective and honest repair should always be the first consideration.
3. We should do no more than prudence demands. In particular we should not fall into the trap of allowing scholarly or artistic ambitions to dictate what is done.

The *Manifesto* also contained another thought which the Society later drew back from, namely that it was better to raise a new building rather than enlarge or alter an old one which had become inconvenient for modern use. This was replaced by an admonition that:

4. Any permanently necessary new work should be clearly distinguishable from the old and should not reproduce any past style.

The admonition that additions should be in 'the natural manner of today' was, however, later removed (see quotation and comment on page 114).

The Venice Charter

The Athens Conference of 1931, organised by the International Museums Office, made the first systematic attempt to set down an international code of practice. A Congress of Architects and Specialists of Historic Buildings, at their second meeting in Venice in 1964 (the first had been in Paris in 1957), approved the text of an International Charter for the Conservation of Monuments and Sites (the *Venice Charter*) superseding the *Athens Charter*.

The *Venice Charter* has appeared in more than one edition, but the differences between them are not significant. The following is the English language text, published by ICOMOS in 1966:

Imbued with a message from the past, the historic monuments of generations of people remain to the present day as living witnesses of their age-old traditions. People are becoming more and more conscious of the unity of human values and regard ancient monuments as a common heritage. The common responsibility to safeguard them for future generations is recognised. It is our duty to hand them on in the full richness of their authenticity.

It is essential that the principles guiding the preservation and restoration of ancient buildings should be agreed and be laid down on an international basis, with each country being responsible for applying the plan within the framework of its own culture and traditions.

By defining these basic principles for the first time, the Athens Charter of 1931 contributed towards the development of an extensive international movement which has assumed concrete form in national documents, in the work of ICOM and UNESCO and in the establishment by the latter of the International Centre for the Study of the Preservation and the Restoration of Cultural Property. Increasing awareness and critical study have been brought to bear on problems which have continually become more complex and varied; now the time has come to examine the Charter afresh in order to make a through study of the principles involved and to enlarge its scope in a new document.

Accordingly, the IInd International Congress of Architects and Technicians of Historic Monuments, which met in Venice from May 25th to 31st 1964, approved the following text:

Definitions

ARTICLE 1. The concept of an historic monument embraces not only the single architectural work but also the urban or rural setting in which is found the evidence of a particular civilisation, a significant development or an historic event. This applies not only to great works of art but also to more modest works of the past which have acquired cultural significance with the passing of time.

ARTICLE 2. The conservation and restoration of monuments must have recourse to all the sciences and techniques which can contribute to the study and safeguarding of the architectural heritage.

Aim

ARTICLE 3. The intention in conserving and restoring monuments is to safeguard them no less as works of art than as historical evidence.

Conservation

ARTICLE 4. It is essential to the conservation of monuments that they be maintained on a permanent basis.

ARTICLE 5. The conservation of monuments is always facilitated by making use of them for some socially useful purpose. Such use is therefore desirable but it must not change the layout or decoration of the building. It is within these limits only that modifications demanded by a change of function should be envisaged and may be permitted.

ARTICLE 6. The conservation of a monument implies preserving a setting which is not out of scale. Wherever the traditional setting exists, it must be kept. No new construction, demolition or modification which would alter the relations of mass and colour must be allowed.

ARTICLE 7. A monument is inseparable from the history to which it bears witness and from the setting in which it occurs. The moving of all or part of a monument cannot be allowed except where the safeguarding of that monument demands it or where it is justified by national or international interests of paramount importance.

ARTICLE 8. Items of sculpture, painting or decoration which form an integral part of a monument may only be removed from it if this is the sole means of ensuring their preservation.

Restoration

ARTICLE 9. The process of restoration is a highly specialised operation. Its aim is to preserve and reveal the aesthetic and historic value of the monument and is based on respect for original material and authentic documents. It must stop at the point where conjecture begins, and in this case moreover any extra work which is indispensable must be distinct from the architectural composition and must bear a contemporary stamp. The restoration in any case must be preceded and followed by an archaeological and historical study of the monument.

ARTICLE 10. Where traditional techniques prove inadequate, the consolidation of a monument can be achieved by the use of any modern technique for conservation and construction, the efficacy of which has been shown by scientific data and proved by experience.

ARTICLE 11. The valid contributions of all periods to the building of a monument must be respected, since unity of style is not the aim of a restoration. When a building includes the superimposed work of different periods, the revealing of the underlying state can only be justified in exceptional circumstances and when what is removed is of little interest and the material which is brought to light is of great historical, archaeological or aesthetic value, and its state of preservation good enough to justify the action. Evaluation of the importance of the elements involved and the decision as to what may be destroyed cannot rest solely on the individual in charge of the work.

ARTICLE 12. Replacements of missing parts must integrate harmoniously with the whole, but at the same time must be distinguishable from the original so that restoration does not falsify the artistic or historic evidence.

ARTICLE 13. Additions cannot be allowed except in so far as they do not detract from the interesting parts of the building, its traditional setting, the balance of its composition and its relation with its surroundings.

Historic sites

ARTICLE 14. The sites of monuments must be the object of special care in order to safeguard their integrity and ensure that they are cleared and presented in a seemly manner. The work of conservation and restoration carried out in such places should be inspired by the principles set forth in the foregoing articles.

Excavations

ARTICLE 15. Excavations should be carried out in accordance with scientific standards and the recommendation defining international principles to be applied in the case of archaeological excavation adopted by UNESCO in 1956.

Ruins must be maintained and measures necessary for the permanent conservation and protection of architectural features and of objects discovered must be taken. Furthermore, every means must be taken to facilitate the understanding of the monument and to reveal it without ever distorting its meaning.

All reconstruction work should however be ruled out a priori. Only anastylosis, that is to say, the re-assembling of existing but dismembered parts can be permitted. The material used for integration should always be recognisable and its use should be the least that will ensure the conservation of a monument and the reinstatement of its form.

Publication

ARTICLE 16. In all works of preservation, restoration or excavation, there should always be precise documentation in the form of analytical and critical reports, illustrated with drawings and photographs.

Every stage of the work of clearing, consolidation, rearrangement and integration, as well as technical and formal features identified during the course of the work, should be included. This record should be placed in the archives of a public institution and made available to research workers. It is recommended that the report should be published.

The Burra Charter

In Burra, South Australia, in 1979, a charter that took *Venice* as its starting point but was tailored to local needs, was adopted by Australia ICOMOS. Subsequently revised, in 1981 and 1988, the latest version was adopted by Australia ICOMOS at its AGM in 1999.

The 1999 *Burra Charter* should not, however, be taken to be a document of significance only in its country of origin. Its clarity of expression, coupled with its common sense approach and its comprehensive set of definitions, has led to its being valued as a practical guide for day-to-day application far beyond Australia. It is now, for example, widely accepted that the 'cultural significance' of a place, as defined by *Burra*, must be fully identified and a detailed conservation plan formulated and justified before any intervention is made.

The concept of cultural significance leads to firm and logical guidelines, such as that 'revealing the fabric of one period at the expense of another can only be justified when what is removed is of slight cultural significance'. The *Charter* draws attention to the less tangible aspects of cultural significance, including those embodied in use. It recognises the importance of the meanings that places have for people and the need for people to be involved in the decision-making processes, particularly those who have strong associations with a place. These, it says 'might be as patrons of the corner store, as workers in a factory or as community guardians of places of special value, whether of indigenous or (other) origin'.

The *Burra Charter* has achieved a more overtly 'official' status than most such codes, in that it has been regularly used by the Australian government to test the grant-worthiness of individual projects.

Note that the Guidelines attached to the *Charter* are important in its application, but are not set out below. At the time of writing the Guidelines were under revision and they were not, for the time being, completely compatible with the 1999 *Charter*. The reader may, however, download the latest Guidelines in full from the Australia ICOMOS web page:

www.icomos.org/australia

Australian ICOMOS Burra Charter 1999
for the Conservation of Places of Cultural Significance

The Burra Charter provides guidance for the conservation and management of places of cultural significance (cultural heritage places), and is based on the knowledge and experience of Australia ICOMOS members. Conservation is an integral part of the management of places of cultural significance and is an ongoing responsibility.

Who is the Charter for?
The Charter sets a standard of practice for those who provide advice, make decisions about, or undertake works to places of cultural significance, including owners, managers and custodians.

Using the Charter
The Charter should be read as a whole. Many articles are interdependent. Articles in the Conservation Principles section are often further developed in the Conservation Processes and Conservation Practice sections. Headings have been included for ease of reading but do not form part of the Charter.
The Charter is self-contained, but aspects of its use and application are further explained in the following Australia ICOMOS documents:
- Guidelines to the Burra Charter: Cultural Significance;
- Guidelines to the Burra Charter: Conservation Policy;
- Guidelines to the Burra Charter: Procedures for Undertaking Studies and Reports;
- Code on the Ethics of Coexistence in Conserving Significant Places.

What places does the Charter apply to?
The Charter can be applied to all types of places of cultural significance including natural, indigenous and historic places with cultural values.
The standards of other organisations may also be relevant. These include the Australian Natural Heritage Charter and the Draft Guidelines for the Protection, Management and Use of Aboriginal and Torres Strait Islander Cultural Heritage Places.

Why conserve?
Places of cultural significance enrich people's lives, often providing a deep and inspirational sense of connection to community and landscape, to the past and to lived experiences. They are historical records, that are important as tangible expressions of Australian identity and experience. Places of cultural significance reflect the diversity of our communities,

telling us about who we are and the past that has formed us and the Australian landscape. They are irreplaceable and precious.

These places of cultural significance must be conserved for present and future generations.

The Burra Charter advocates a cautious approach to change: do as much as necessary to care for the place and to make it useable, but otherwise change it as little as possible so that its cultural significance is retained.

Article 1	Definitions	Explanatory Notes
	For the purpose of this Charter:	These notes do not form part of the Charter and may be added to by Australia ICOMOS.
1.1	*Place* means site, area, land, landscape, building or other work, group of buildings or other works, and may include components, contents, spaces and views.	The concept of place should be broadly interpreted. The elements described in Article 1.1 may include memorials, trees, gardens, parks, places of historical events, urban areas, towns, industrial places, archaeological sites and spiritual and religious places.
1.2	*Cultural significance* means aesthetic, historic, scientific, social or spiritual value for past, present or future generations. Cultural significance is embodied in the *place* itself, its *fabric, setting, use, associations, meanings, records, related places and related objects.* Places may have a range of values for different individuals or groups.	The term cultural significance is synonymous with heritage significance and cultural heritage value. Cultural significance may change as a result of the continuing history of the place. Understanding of cultural significance may change as a result of new information.
1.3	*Fabric* means all the physical material of the *place* including components, fixtures, contents, and objects.	Fabric includes building interiors and sub-surface remains, as well as excavated material. Fabric may define spaces and these may be important elements of the significance of the place.
1.4	*Conservation* means all the processes of looking after a *place* so as to retain its *cultural significance*.	

1.5 *Maintenance* means the continuous protective care of the *fabric* and *setting* of a *place*, and is to be distinguished from repair. Repair involves *restoration* or *reconstruction*.

The distinctions referred to, for example in relation to roof gutters, are
• maintenance – regular inspection and cleaning of gutters;
• repair involving restoration – returning of dislodged gutters;
• repair involving reconstruction – replacing decayed gutters.

1.6 *Preservation* means maintaining the *fabric* of a *place* in its existing state and retarding deterioration.

It is recognised that all places and their components change over time at varying rates.

1.7 *Restoration* means returning the existing *fabric* of a *place* to a known earlier state by removing accretions or by reassembling existing components without the introduction of new material.

1.8 *Reconstruction* means returning a *place* to a known earlier state and is distinguished from *restoration* by the introduction of new material into the *fabric*.

New material may include recycled material salvaged from other places. This should not be to the detriment of any place of cultural significance.

1.9 *Adaptation* means modifying a *place* to suit the existing *use* or a proposed use.

1.10 *Use* means the functions of a place, as well as the activities and practices that may occur at the place.

1.11 *Compatible use* means a *use* which respects the *cultural significance* of a *place*. Such a use involves no, or minimal, impact on cultural significance.

1.12 *Setting* means the area around a *place*, which may include the visual catchment.

1.13 *Related place* means a *place* that contributes to the *cultural significance* of another place.

1.14 *Related object* means an object that contributes to the *cultural significance* of a *place* but is not at the place.

1.15 *Associations* mean the special connections that exist between people and a *place*.

Associations may include social or spiritual values and cultural responsibilities for a place.

1.16 *Meanings* denote what a *place* signifies, indicates, evokes or expresses.

Meanings generally relate to intangible aspects such as symbolic qualities and memories.

1.17 *Interpretation* means all the ways of presenting the *cultural significance* of a *place*.

Interpretation may be a combination of the treatment of the fabric (e.g. maintenance, restoration, reconstruction); the use of and activities at the place; and the use of introduced explanatory material.

Conservation Principles

Article 2 Conservation and management

2.1 *Places* of *cultural significance* should be conserved.

2.2 The aim of *conservation* is to retain the *cultural significance* of a place.

2.3 *Conservation* is an integral part of good management of *places* of *cultural significance*.

2.4 *Places* of *cultural significance* should be safeguarded and not put at risk or left in a vulnerable state.

Article 3 Cautious approach

3.1 *Conservation* is based on a respect for the existing *fabric, use, associations* and *meanings*. It requires a cautious approach of changing as much as necessary but as little as possible.

The traces of additions, alterations and earlier treatments to the fabric of a place are evidence of its history and uses which may be part of its significance. Conservation action should assist and not impede their understanding.

3.2 Changes to a *place* should not distort the physical or other evidence it provides, nor be based on conjecture.

Article 4   Knowledge, skills and techniques

4.1   *Conservation* should make use of all the knowledge, skills and disciplines which can contribute to the study and care of the *place*.

4.2   Traditional techniques and materials are preferred for the *conservation* of significant *fabric*. In some circumstances modern techniques and materials which offer substantial conservation benefits may be appropriate.

The use of modern materials and techniques must be supported by firm scientific evidence or by a body of experience.

Article 5   Values

5.1   *Conservation* of a *place* should identify and take into consideration all aspects of cultural and natural significance without unwarranted emphasis on any one value at the expense of others.

Conservation of places with natural significance is explained in the Australian Natural Heritage Charter. This Charter defines natural significance to mean the importance of ecosystems, biological diversity and geodiversity for their existence value, or for present or future generations in terms of their scientific, social, aesthetic and life-support value.

5.2   Relative degrees of *cultural significance* may lead to different *conservation* actions at a place.

A cautious approach is needed, as understanding of cultural significance may change. This article should not be used to justify actions which do not retain cultural significance.

Article 6   Burra Charter Process

6.1   The *cultural significance* of a *place* and other issues affecting its future are best understood by a sequence of collecting and analysing information before making decisions. Understanding cultural significance comes first, then development of policy and finally management of the place in accordance with the policy.

The Burra Charter process, or sequence of investigations, decisions and actions, is illustrated in the accompanying flowchart.

6.2   The policy for managing a *place* must be based on an understanding of its *cultural significance*.

6.3   Policy development should also include consideration of other factors affecting the future of a *place* such as the owner's needs, resources, external constraints and its physical condition.

Article 7   Use

7.1   Where the *use* of a *place* is of *cultural significance* it should be retained.

7.2   A *place* should have a *compatible use*.

The policy should identify a use or combination of uses or constraints on uses that retain the cultural significance of the place. New use of a place should involve minimal change, to significant fabric and use; should respect associations and meanings; and where appropriate should provide for continuation of practices which contribute to the cultural significance of the place.

Article 8   Setting

Conservation requires the retention of an appropriate visual *setting* and other relationships that contribute to the *cultural significance* of the *place*. New construction, demolition, intrusions or other changes which would adversely affect the setting or relationships are not appropriate.

Aspects of the visual setting may include use, siting, bulk, form, scale, character, colour, texture and materials. Other relationships, such as historical connections, may contribute to interpretation, appreciation, enjoyment or experience of the place.

Article 9   Location

9.1   The physical location of a *place* is part of its *cultural significance*. A building, work or other component of a place should remain in its historical location. Relocation is generally unacceptable unless this is the sole practical means of ensuring its survival.

9.2 Some buildings, works or other components of *places* were designed to be readily removable or already have a history of relocation. Provided such buildings, works or other components do not have significant links with their present location, removal may be appropriate.

9.3 If any building, work or other component is moved, it should be moved to an appropriate location and given an appropriate *use*. Such action should not be to the detriment of any *place* of *cultural significance*.

Article 10 Contents

Contents, fixtures and objects which contribute to the *cultural significance* of a *place* should be retained at that place. Their removal is unacceptable unless it is: the sole means of ensuring their security and *preservation*; on a temporary basis for treatment or exhibition; for cultural reasons; for health and safety; or to protect the place. Such contents, fixtures and objects should be returned where circumstances permit and it is culturally appropriate.

Article 11 Related places and objects

The contribution which *related places* and *related objects* make to the *cultural significance* of the *place* should be retained.

Article 12 Participation

Conservation, interpretation and management of a *place* should provide for the participation of people for whom the place has special *associations* and *meanings*, or who have social, spiritual or other cultural responsibilities for the place.

Article 13   Co-existence of cultural values

Co-existence of cultural values should be recognised, respected and encouraged, especially in cases where they conflict.

For some places, conflicting cultural values may affect policy development and management decisions. In this article, the term cultural values refers to those beliefs which are important to a cultural group, including but not limited to political, religious, spiritual and moral beliefs. This is broader than values associated with cultural significance.

Conservation Processes

Article 14   Conservation processes

Conservation may, according to circumstance, include the processes of: retention or reintroduction of a *use*; retention of *associations* and *meanings; maintenance, preservation, restoration, reconstruction, adaptation* and *interpretation*; and will commonly include a combination of more than one of these.

There may be circumstances where no action is required to achieve conservation.

Article 15   Change

15.1   Change may be necessary to retain *cultural significance*, but is undesirable where it reduces cultural significance. The amount of change to a *place* should be guided by the *cultural significance* of the place and its appropriate *interpretation*.

When change is being considered, a range of options should be explored to seek the option which minimises the reduction of cultural significance.

15.2   Changes which reduce *cultural significance* should be reversible, and be reversed when circumstances permit.

Reversible changes should be considered temporary. Non-reversible change should only be used as a last resort and should not prevent future conservation action.

15.3   Demolition of significant *fabric* of a *place* is generally not acceptable. However, in some cases minor demolition may be appropriate as part of *conservation*. Removed significant fabric should be reinstated when circumstances permit.

15.4 The contributions of all aspects of *cultural significance* of a *place* should be respected. If a place includes *fabric, uses, associations* or *meanings* of different periods, or different aspects of cultural significance, emphasising or interpreting one period or aspect at the expense of another can only be justified when what is left out, removed or diminished is of slight cultural significance and that which is emphasised or interpreted is of much greater cultural significance.

Article 16   Maintenance

Maintenance is fundamental to *conservation* and should be undertaken where fabric is of *cultural significance* and its *maintenance* is necessary to retain that *cultural significance*.

Article 17   Preservation

Preservation is appropriate where the existing *fabric* or its condition constitutes evidence of *cultural significance*, or where insufficient evidence is available to allow other *conservation* processes to be carried out.

Preservation protects fabric without obscuring the evidence of its construction and use. The process should always be applied:
- where the evidence of the fabric is of such significance that it should not be altered;
- where insufficient investigation has been carried out to permit policy decisions to be taken in accord with Articles 26 to 28.

New work (e.g. stabilisation) may be carried out in association with preservation when its purpose is the physical protection of the fabric and when it is consistent with Article 22.

Article 18   Restoration and reconstruction

Restoration and *reconstruction* should reveal culturally significant aspects of the *place*.

Article 19   Restoration

Restoration is appropriate only if there is sufficient evidence of an earlier state of the *fabric*.

Article 20   Reconstruction

20.1   *Reconstruction* is appropriate only where a *place* is incomplete through damage or alteration, and only where there is sufficient evidence to reproduce an earlier state of the *fabric*. In rare cases, reconstruction may also be appropriate as part of a *use* or practice that retains the *cultural significance* of the place.

20.2   *Reconstruction* should be identifiable on close inspection or through additional *interpretation*.

Article 21   Adaptation

Adaptation must be limited to that which is essential to a use for the *place* determined in accordance with Articles 6 and 7.

21.1   *Adaptation* is acceptable only where the adaptation has minimal impact on the *cultural significance* of the *place*.

Adaptation may involve the introduction of new services, or a new use, or changes to safeguard the place.

21.2   *Adaptation* should involve minimal change to significant fabric, achieved only after considering alternatives.

Article 22   New work

22.1   New work such as additions to the *place* may be acceptable where it does not distort or obscure the *cultural significance* of the place, or detract from its *interpretation* and appreciation.

New work may be sympathetic if its siting, bulk, form, scale, character, colour, texture and material are similar to the existing fabric, but imitation should be avoided.

22.2   New work should be readily identifiable as such.

Article 23   Conserving use

Continuing, modifying or reinstating a significant *use* may be appropriate and preferred forms of *conservation*.

These may require changes to significant *fabric* but they should be minimised. In some cases, continuing a significant use or practice may involve substantial new work.

Article 24   Retaining associations and meanings

24.1   Significant *associations* between people and a *place* should be respected, retained and not obscured. Opportunities for the *interpretation*, commemoration and celebration of these associations should be investigated and implemented.

For many places associations will be linked to use.

24.2   Significant *meanings*, including spiritual values, of a *place* should be respected. Opportunities for the continuation or revival of these meanings should be investigated and implemented.

Article 25   Interpretation

The *cultural significance* of many *places* is not readily apparent, and should be explained by *interpretation*. Interpretation should enhance understanding and enjoyment, and be culturally appropriate.

Article 26   Applying the Burra Charter process

26.1   Work on a *place* should be preceded by studies to understand the place which should include analysis of physical, documentary, oral and other evidence, drawing on appropriate knowledge, skills and disciplines.

The results of studies should be up to date, regularly reviewed and revised as necessary.

26.2   Written statements of *cultural significance* and policy for the *place* should be prepared, justified and accompanied by supporting evidence. The statements of significance and policy should be incorporated into a management plan for the place.

Statements of significance and policy should be kept up to date by regular review and revision as necessary. The management plan may deal with other matters related to the management of the place.

26.3   Groups and individuals with *associations* with a *place* as well as those involved in its management should be provided with opportunities to contribute to and participate in understanding the *cultural significance* of the place. Where appropriate they should also have opportunities to participate in its *conservation* and management.

Article 27   Managing change

27.1   The impact of proposed changes on the *cultural significance* of a *place* should be analysed with reference to the statement of significance and the policy for managing the place. It may be necessary to modify proposed changes following analysis to better retain cultural significance.

27.2   Existing *fabric, use, associations* and *meanings* should be adequately recorded before any changes are made to the *place*.

Article 28   Disturbance of fabric

Disturbance of significant *fabric* for study, or to obtain evidence, should be minimised. Study of a *place* by any disturbance of the fabric, including archaeological excavation, should only be undertaken to provide data essential for decisions on the *conservation* of the place, or to obtain important evidence about to be lost or made inaccessible. Investigation of a *place* which requires disturbance of the *fabric*, apart from that necessary to make decisions, may be appropriate provided that it is consistent with the policy for the place. Such investigation should be based on important research questions which have potential to substantially add to knowledge, which cannot be answered in other ways and which minimises disturbance of significant fabric.

Article 29   Responsibility for decisions

The organisations and individuals responsible for management decisions should be named and specific responsibility taken for each such decision.

Article 30   Direction, supervision and implementation

Competent direction and supervision should be maintained at all stages, and any changes should be implemented by people with appropriate knowledge and skills.

Article 31   Documenting evidence and decisions

A log of new evidence and additional decisions should be kept.

Article 32   Records

32.1   The records associated with the *conservation* of a *place* should be placed in a permanent archive and made publicly available, subject to requirements of security and privacy, and where this is culturally appropriate.

32.2   Records about the history of a *place* should be protected and made publicly available, subject to requirements of security and privacy, and where this is culturally appropriate.

Article 33 Removed fabric

Significant *fabric* which has been removed from a *place* including contents, fixtures and objects, should be catalogued, and protected in accordance with its *cultural significance*.
Where possible and culturally appropriate, removed significant fabric including contents, fixtures and objects, should be kept at the place.

Article 34 Resources

Adequate resources should be provided for *conservation*.

The best conservation often involves the least work and can be inexpensive.

Words in italics are defined in Article 1.

© Australia ICOMOS 1999

Background to Australia ICOMOS

Australia ICOMOS' mission is to raise standards, encourage debate and generate innovative ideas in cultural heritage conservation.

lCOMOS (International Council on Monuments and Sites) is a non-government organisation that promotes expertise in the conservation of cultural heritage. Formed in 1965, it is primarily concerned with the philosophy, terminology, methodology and techniques of conservation. ICOMOS has national committees in over 100 countries and is closely linked to UNESCO.

Australia ICOMOS, formed in 1976, links public authorities, institutions and individuals involved in the study and conservation of all places of cultural significance.

Australia ICOMOS' goals are:

International: Participate in international activities, both within and beyond the ICOMOS international family.

Conservation Philosophy and policy: Ensure that Australia 1COMOS leads conservation philosophy end practice for culturally significant places.

Education and Communication: Promote understanding of the cultural significance of places, raising conservation standards through education and communication programs.

Advocacy: Inform key decision-makers of Australia ICOMOS' aims and influence their adoption of best conservation philosophy and practice.

Membership: Develop, maintain and support a broad-based membership.

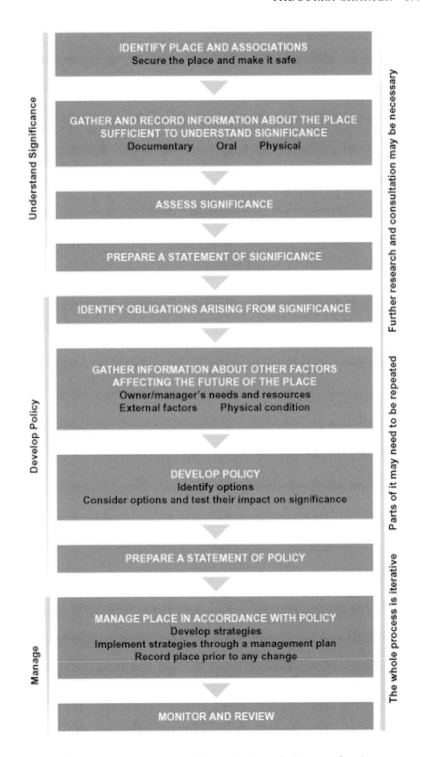

The Burra Charter Process. Sequence of investigations, decisions and actions

APPENDIX 5

The Canadian Code of Ethics

From a number of North American codes and charters I have selected one which seems to me to adopt a particularly practical and reasonable outlook. It has the particular interest of encompassing relations with other professionals and with owners as well as embodying a clear conservation philosophy. A *Code of Ethics for those Involved in Conservation* was drawn up in Ottawa in 1985 and first published in 1986. The third edition, published in 2000 is the joint work of the Canadian Association for the Conservation of Cultural Property (CAC) and the Canadian Association of Professional Conservators.

The *Code* is designed for the special conditions of Canada (where building conservation has never been the exclusive preserve of one profession) and provides plain language guidance, rather than merely echoing worthy sentiments. The document opens with the statement that it is 'intended to serve both as a guideline for use by conservators and as an outline of the ethical obligations of conservators for use by their clients, colleagues and employers'. Like the *Burra Charter,* the *Code* is careful to define the terms it uses. Note particularly the glossary definition of *reconstruction*, which is somewhat farther-reaching than the apparently similar concept in *Burra*. Extensive re-creations are clearly not regarded as taboo in a country hungry for symbols of its own beginnings.

The main provisions of the *Code* are given here, slightly edited, with the omission of some preliminary and peripheral material, viz. the publication history, the contents list, a list of equivalent terms in French (essential in bilingual Canada) and the bibliography (whose references are mainly to North American journals).

Asterisked * words indicate an entry in the glossary.

The complete text can be downloaded from the CAC website: www.cac-accr.ca/

Code of Ethics

The fundamental role of the conservation professional is to preserve and to restore, as appropriate, cultural property for present and future generations. The following are principles of ethical behaviour for those involved in the conservation of cultural property:

I. It is the responsibility of the conservation professional*, acting alone or with others, to strive constantly to maintain a balance between the need in society to use a cultural property*, and to ensure the preservation* of that cultural property.

II. In the conservation* of cultural property, all actions of the conservation professional must be governed by an informed respect for the integrity of the property, including physical, conceptual, historical and aesthetic considerations.

III. The conservation professional shall strive to attain the highest possible standards in all aspects of conservation, including preventive conservation*, examination*, documentation*, research, treatment* and education.

IV. The conservation professional shall seek to prevent damage and deterioration to a cultural property under his/her care by implementing, or by recommending to the owner, appropriate preventive conservation measures.

V. The conservation professional shall recognize his or her limitations and the special skills and knowledge of others.

VI. The conservation professional shall continue to develop knowledge and skills with the aim of improving the quality of his/her professional work.

VII. The conservation professional shall contribute to the evolution and growth of the profession by sharing experience and information with colleagues.

VIII. The conservation professional shall act with honesty and integrity in all professional relationships, recognize the rights of all colleagues and respect the profession as a whole.

IX. The conservation professional shall seek to promote an awareness and understanding of conservation through communication with those who have a vested interest in the cultural property, with other professionals and with members of the public.

X. The conservation professional has an obligation to comply with and to promote an understanding of this *Code of Ethics*.

Guidance for Practice

An interpretation of the principles stated in the *Code of Ethics*.

Professional Standards in the Conservation of Cultural Property

GENERAL OBLIGATIONS

1. Shared Responsibility

The care and treatment* of a cultural property* is the shared responsibility of the owner*, the conservation professional* and when applicable, the originator*.

2. Respect for the Integrity of the Cultural Property

When conserving a cultural property, the conservation professional shall respect the integrity of the cultural property by endeavouring to preserve its material composition and culturally significant qualities through minimal intervention. The original intention, usage, history and evidence of provenance of the property must be respected. This respect for the integrity of the cultural property shall be based upon the study of the cultural property and on consultations with the owner and, when applicable, the originator. When relevant, other authorities or documentary sources should be consulted.

3. Standard of Conservation* Work

While circumstances may limit both the resources allocated to a particular situation and the extent of the work, the quality of work that the conservation professional performs shall not be compromised, regardless of any opinion held with respect to the value or quality of the cultural property.

4. Documentation*

The conservation professional shall document his/her work by recording all essential details of the conservation of a cultural property. The extent and type of documentation will vary with the nature of the cultural property and conservation work required. Documentation is part of the history of the cultural property and shall be produced and maintained in as permanent a manner as is practical. Documentation shall be available for appropriate access when this access does not contravene confidentiality.

5. Recognition of Limitations

The conservation professional shall carry out only that work which is within the limits of his/her professional competence and facilities. When a conservation professional is asked to provide a service beyond the limits of his/her competence, the assistance of a qualified professional shall be sought or the work shall be referred or subcontracted to a qualified professional.

6. Professional Development

The conservation professional shall strive to improve his/her knowledge and skills and keep abreast of current developments through continuing study and through communication with conservation professionals and others.

7. Preventive Conservation*

Preventive conservation is a primary objective of the conservation professional and must be considered prior to direct intervention with the cultural property. The conservation professional shall strive to ensure appropriate conditions of storage, display, use and handling of a cultural property, or shall provide guidance for others to do so.

8. Safekeeping of Cultural Property

The conservation professional should ensure working, storage and transportation conditions designed to protect cultural property while in his or her care.

EXAMINATION

9. Examination*

The conservation professional shall make a thorough examination of the cultural property and shall document this examination before performing any conservation treatment. This examination includes a determination of its structure and materials and an assessment of its condition, in particular, the extent of deterioration, alteration and loss. He/she shall study relevant historical and technical records. Where necessary, the conservation professional should initiate analyses of materials and undertake research into historical, conceptual and technical aspects of the cultural property.

10. Risks of Examination

Before undertaking any examination which may result in a change in the cultural property, the conservation professional shall establish the necessity for such an examination and receive permission to proceed from the owner.

11. Sampling

In cases where sample material must be taken from a cultural property, prior consent must be obtained from the owner. Only a minimum of sample material shall be removed, and a record of sample removal shall be kept. Where relevant, and with the agreement of the owner, material removed from a cultural property should be retained as part of the documentation of that cultural property.

12. Documentation of Examination

The conservation professional shall prepare an examination report (alternatively called 'condition report') that shall identify the cultural property, include all relevant information on its structure, materials, history and condition, and provide the date of the examination. The conservation professional shall provide a copy of the examination report to the owner.

CONSERVATION TREATMENT

13. Necessity and Extent of Treatment

The conservation professional shall only recommend or undertake treatment that is necessary to, and appropriate for, the conservation of the cultural property. Conversely, a conservation professional shall not intentionally omit to recommend an essential treatment. When non-intervention best serves to promote the preservation* of the cultural property, it is appropriate that no treatment be performed.

14. Treatment Proposal

On the basis of the examination, the conservation professional shall report his/her findings and recommendations in writing to the owner, including justification for and the objectives of the treatment, an estimate of resources required, alternative approaches if feasible, and the potential risks of treatment. The treatment proposal is submitted in order to fully inform the owner and to obtain consent to proceed. For large groups of similar objects (for example library collections, archaeological finds), a treatment proposal may be written for the group as a whole. Any significant changes to the proposed treatment shall be conveyed to the owner and consent must be received before the conservation professional carries out the revised treatment.

15. Documentation of Treatment

Treatment records shall include the date of the treatment, a description of the interventions and of the materials used (with their composition, where known), observations, as well as any details of the structure, materials, condition or relevant history of the cultural property that have been revealed during treatment. From these records a summary shall be prepared in the form of a treatment report. The conservation professional shall provide the owner with this report and shall stress the importance of maintaining the report as part of the history of the cultural property.

16. Techniques and Materials

The conservation professional shall endeavour to use only techniques and materials which, to the best of current knowledge, meet the objectives of the treatment and have the least adverse effect on the cultural property. Ideally, the conservation professional shall use materials that can be most easily and most completely removed with minimal risk to any original part. Similarly, these techniques and materials should not impede future treatment or examination.

17. Removal or Alteration of Material

No aspect of a cultural property should be altered nor should material be removed from it without justification. When such removal or alteration is required, those aspects or materials shall first be documented in their existing state. Where relevant, and with the agreement of the owner, material removed from an object shall be retained as part of the documentation of a cultural property.

18. Restoration* and Reconstruction*

Restoration and reconstruction are means of re-establishing culturally significant qualities of a cultural property. If undertaken they shall be fully documented and shall be carried out without fraudulent intent and to the minimum extent necessary. The presence and extent of any restoration or reconstruction must be detectable, though they need not be conspicuous.

19. Reformatting*

Reformatting is an appropriate intervention for cultural property which is valued exclusively for its information content and where, despite current conservation practices, future retrieval of this information may not be possible.

20. Reproduction or Detailed Recording

When a cultural property is inherently unstable or when its social use is incompatible with its preservation, the conservation professional shall recommend a reproduction or a detailed recording as appropriate to the situation. The conservation professional shall outline suitable options that meet the need for content retention and that will result, during the reproduction or recording, in the least alteration to the original. A reproduction shall be clearly and easily identified as such.

SUBSEQUENT CARE

21. Subsequent Care

The conservation professional shall advise the owner on the requirements for subsequent care of the cultural property, which may include specifications for shipping and handling, storage, display and maintenance.

EMERGENCY SITUATIONS

22. Emergency Situations

The conservation professional shall endeavour to be prepared for emergency situations or to undertake emergency response planning according to currently accepted practice. This includes consultation with the owner and, when applicable, with the originator in order to establish the extent of, or priority for, recovery. In an emergency, the conservation professional shall render all assistance practicable with due respect given, as far as possible, to the guidelines in this document. If a departure from normal practice is necessary, the conservation professional shall take care to advise the owner or appropriate authority and should recommend subsequent actions. During or subsequent to the emergency situation, the conservation professional shall document the actions taken.

PROFESSIONAL CONDUCT

Relationship with the Owner

23. Relationship with the Owner

The conservation professional shall strive to establish a relationship with the owner based on mutual trust and respect. He/she shall communicate openly and clearly with the owner so that there is a thorough understanding of risks and responsibilities, and that agreements between the two parties reflect shared decisions and realistic expectations.

24. Confidentiality

The conservation professional shall consider relationships with an owner as confidential. Information pertaining to the cultural property derived from examination, scientific investigation or treatment of the cultural property shall not be published or otherwise made public without permission of the owner, unless failure to convey the information would support an illegal or an unethical act. The conservation professional shall not take personal, financial or other advantage of this information nor allow others to take advantage of this information unless the owner consents.

25. Contract

The conservation professional may enter into contractual agreements with individuals, institutions, businesses, or government agencies provided that such agreements do not conflict with the terms and intent of the *Code of Ethics and Guidance for Practice*. It is prudent to obtain written contracts in order to avoid misunderstandings and to support the legal rights and responsibilities of the parties involved. Where possible, the agreement with the client should specify the following: the work to be done, its objectives and justification; the possible effects and outcome of the work; the basis for fees or estimate of fees; the extent and type of documentation; the expected completion date; method of handling; whether any work is to be delegated or subcontracted.

26. Fees

The conservation professional shall ensure at all times that conservation services are carried out in a financially responsible manner with due regard for fairness to the client and with respect for the profession. Fees charged for services provided to the private sector shall take into account all costs related to providing the service, the ability and experience of the conservation professionals involved, and the degree of responsibility assumed. The conservation professional shall establish a consistent fee structure which shall not vary according to the value of the cultural property. Agreement on fees shall be obtained from the client prior to providing conservation services.

27. Consent of the Owner

The informed consent of the owner must be obtained prior to a direct intervention which may result in a change in the cultural property. It is prudent to obtain the owner's consent in writing in order to avoid misunderstandings and to support the legal rights and responsibilities of the parties involved.

28. Request for a Second Opinion

If, for any reason, before or during treatment, the owner requests the opinion of another conservation professional, this request shall be respected by the original conservation professional. The conservation professional should assist the owner in obtaining a second opinion.

29. In Case of Disagreement

Should the conservation professional and the owner disagree over a proposed treatment or care of a cultural property, they should review the situation, if necessary in consultation with other specialists in the field, to ensure that the nature of the problems and implications of the treatment or care are fully understood. The conservation professional maintains the right of refusal to undertake any treatment or procedure which he/she considers to be contrary to the terms and intent of the *Code of Ethics and Guidance for Practice.*

Relationship with Other Professionals, Trainees and Members of the Public

30. Communication

To further the development of the profession, a conservation professional should, where possible, share with colleagues information gained from research, examination, preventive conservation activities or treatment. The peer review system shall be encouraged as part of professional publishing practice.

31. False Information

The conservation professional shall not knowingly be party to the dissemination of false or misleading information pertaining to any of the following: cultural property, its age, origin, or authenticity; professional or business relationships; conservation materials, procedures or services.

32. Advertising

Advertising and other representations by the conservation professional shall present an accurate description of credentials and services.

33. Public Education

The conservation professional shall promote an awareness and understanding of conservation through communication with, and dissemination of appropriate information to, those who have a vested interest in the cultural property, other professionals and members of the general public. Prior to providing training or detailed information that pertains to conservation treatments, the conservation professional shall set, where necessary, appropriate criteria for qualifications and experience of the participants.

34. Training

The conservation professional should endeavour to become involved in the instruction of trainees, but only within the limits of his/her knowledge and ability, and the time and technical facilities available. The objectives and obligations of both the trainer and the trainee should be clearly stated and mutually agreed upon in writing, and should include such items as terms of payment, anticipated length of training and areas of competence to be taught.

35. Delegating and Subcontracting

The conservation professional is responsible for delegated or subcontracted work on cultural property. This includes work delegated to other conservation professionals, trainees, volunteers and other individuals. Work shall not be delegated or subcontracted unless the individual has the appropriate qualifications to execute the work. The conservation professional shall provide direct supervision unless he/she has sufficient knowledge of the individual to be confident that the work will be of a high standard. The conservation professional shall ensure that appropriate remuneration is given for subcontracted work. The conservation professional shall inform the owner whether delegating or subcontracting is to occur.

36. Acknowledgment
The conservation professional shall ensure that work produced by a colleague (trainee, contractor, co-worker) is acknowledged, where appropriate, in documentation, publications and presentations of that work. The author's consent must be obtained before the dissemination of unpublished research or reports.

37. References and Referrals
The conservation professional shall only provide a reference for an individual if he/she has personal knowledge of the competence and experience of that individual. The conservation professional shall make referrals only to accredited professionals, or to professionals in which he/she has knowledge of their competence. When acting on behalf of an employer, a conservation professional employed by a public institution shall make referrals in a manner which best meets the needs of the client and which respects fair competition by providing a list of qualified professionals.

38. Comments on the Work of Another Conservation Professional
The conservation professional shall not volunteer adverse judgement or comment on the work of another conservation professional, except where non-disclosure will result in damage to the cultural property. All comments should be based on facts and personal knowledge rather than on hearsay. If such comments are warranted, it is best to first discuss the matter directly with the person concerned; further comment and discussion belong in an appropriate forum.

39. Conflict of Interest
The conservation professional shall not enter knowingly into contractual or other working arrangements or agreements which place the conservation professional in a position of conflict of interest. The conservation professional shall be especially mindful of the considerable potential for conflict of interest in activities such as authentication, appraisal or art dealing. The potential for conflict of interest also exists when a conservation professional employed by an institution, studio, workshop or similar business engages in freelance conservation work.

40. Freelance Work

A conservation professional taking on freelance conservation work when employed by an institution, studio, workshop or similar business shall not trade on the name of the employer and shall make it clear that he/she is acting on behalf of him/herself. He/she shall not solicit or accept offers of freelance work when he/she is acting as a representative of his/her employer. He/she shall inform the employer that he/she is engaged in freelance work.

41. Laws and Regulations

The conservation professional shall comply with laws and regulations that have a bearing on his/her professional activity. Among the laws and regulations which may apply, are those which pertain to copyright, sacred and religious material, human remains, excavated objects, stolen property, endangered species, fair business practices, conflict of interest, and occupational health and safety.

42. Illicit Materials

When a conservation professional knows, or has reason to believe, that he/she is being asked to work on a cultural property that has been obtained through theft or unlicensed excavation, or that has been imported illegally into Canada, it is his/her duty to make this known to the relevant authorities.

43. Safety

The conservation professional shall comply with safety regulations and use techniques and materials in a responsible manner to minimize hazards to people and the environment. He/she shall be aware of the safety issues associated with materials and procedures and adjust his/her work accordingly. The conservation professional shall make this information available to others who may be affected. The conservation professional shall inform the owner of known hazards that are inherent to the cultural property or to its normal use. He/she shall ensure that a cultural property intended for use meets safety and regulatory requirements.

44. Conduct

Adherence to the *Code of Ethics and Guidance for Practice* is a matter of personal and professional responsibility. Should a situation arise which is not clearly covered by these guidelines, the conservation professional shall adhere to the intent of the *Code of Ethics*

Glossary

Conservation:
All actions aimed at the safeguarding of cultural property for the future. The purpose of conservation is to study, record, retain and restore the culturally significant qualities of the cultural property as embodied in its physical and chemical nature, with the least possible intervention. Conservation includes the following: examination, documentation, preventive conservation, preservation, treatment, restoration and reconstruction.

Conservation Professional:
For the purposes of this document, conservation professional refers to any person who has the education, knowledge, ability and experience to formulate and carry out conservation activities in accordance with an ethical code such as this *Code of Ethics and Guidance for Practice*. The term, therefore, includes practising conservators (who are normally designated according to areas of specialization, e.g. paintings conservator, textile conservator, architectural conservator) as well as conservation scientists, conservation technicians, conservation educators, conservation managers and conservation consultants.

Cultural Property:
Objects that are judged by society, or by some of its members, to be of historical, artistic, social or scientific importance. Cultural property can be classified into two major categories:
1 Movable objects such as works of art, artifacts, books, archival material and other objects of natural, historical or archaeological origin.
2 Immovable objects such as monuments, architecture, archaeological sites and structures of historical or artistic interest.

Documentation:
All of the records, written and pictorial, accumulated during the examination and treatment of a cultural property. Where applicable, documentation includes the examination records and report, treatment proposal, owner consent, the treatment records and report, the recommendations for subsequent care, samples taken from the cultural property and relevant correspondence. The purpose of documentation is:
• to record the condition of the cultural property;
• to record in formation revealed during examination or other conservation activities that assists in the understanding of the cultural property;
• to record the changes to the property due to conservation activities, and the justification for those changes;

- to provide information helpful to future care and treatment of the cultural property;
- to record agreements or understandings between the conservation professional and the owner; and
- to provide documents that can be made available if and when required for legal purposes.

Examination:
All activities carried out to determine the structure, materials, relevant history and condition of a cultural property, including the extent of deterioration, alteration and loss. Examination also includes analyses and study of relevant material, as well as the study of relevant historical and contemporary information.

Originator:
For the purpose of this document, the originator is either:
1   The person(s) who designed or created the cultural property, or
2   The person (s) representing the creator or designer of the cultural property by legal, moral or spiritual right.

Owner:
For the purpose of this document, the owner is either:
1   The person(s) having legal ownership of the cultural property, or his/her authorized agent, or
2   The person(s), such as the museum director, curator, archivist or librarian, exercising professional custodianship over a cultural property.

Preservation:
All actions taken to retard deterioration of, or to prevent damage to, cultural property. Preservation involves management of the environment and of the conditions of use, and may include treatment in order to maintain a cultural property, as nearly as possible, in a stable physical condition. With respect to material valued exclusively for its information content, for example some archival material, preservation may include reformatting.

Preventive Conservation:
All actions taken to mitigate deterioration and damage to cultural property. This is achieved through the formulation and implementation of policies and procedures in areas such as lighting, environmental conditions, air quality, integrated pest management; handling, packing and transport, exhibition, storage, maintenance, use, security; fire protection, and emergency preparedness and response.

Reconstruction:
All actions taken to re-create, in whole or in part, a cultural property, based upon historical, literary, graphic, pictorial, archaeological and scientific evidence. Reconstruction is aimed at promoting an understanding of a cultural property, and is based on little or no original material but clear evidence of a former state.

Reformatting:
All actions taken to transfer onto another medium, the information contained within a cultural property valued exclusively for its information content (for example, archival electronic media).

Restoration:
All actions taken to modify the existing materials and structure of a cultural property to represent a known earlier state. The aim of restoration is to reveal the culturally significant qualities of a cultural property. Restoration is based on respect for the remaining original material and clear evidence of the earlier state.

Treatment:
All direct interventions carried out on the cultural property with the aim of retarding further deterioration or aiding in the interpretation of the cultural property. A treatment may range from minimal stabilization to extensive restoration or reconstruction.

The Philosophical Background to Listing in Britain

Chapter 4 discussed the kinds of buildings that recommend themselves as being so 'special' as to merit protection. Mention was made in that chapter of the instructions given to the first Ministry of Town and Country Planning Investigators in 1946, as they set out across largely uncharted territory to compile the 'statutory lists' of buildings of special architectural or historic interest required by Section 42 of the Town and Country Planning Act of 1944.

Although a number of well-researched, but informal, lists of historic buildings had been in progress for many years (by, for example, the London County Council, the Manchester Society of Architects and the Surrey County Council) the national statutory lists did not have an easy birth. The 1944 Bill provided for the re-enactment and extension of the existing (1932) building preservation order provisions, but civil servants advised the Minister of Town and Country Planning against the inclusion of listing provisions in a bill designed mainly to deal with post-war reconstruction. The time was, nevertheless, clearly ripe and the need demonstrably urgent. The necessary clauses were, in the end, inserted as a result of a private member's amendment, proposed with the Minister's agreement and carried by a substantial majority. The Act required formal notice to be given of proposals to demolish or alter buildings included in the statutory lists (which had yet to be created).

Parliament had, thus, willed the end but a succession of governments were reluctant to provide the means. Lack of commitment led to the initial lists taking well over twenty years to complete and they were frequently criticised both for what they protected and what they failed to protect. Nearly all of the criticisms should, in fairness, be directed at those who administered the protective processes at central and local government level, rather than at the under-resourced listers. For the first quarter century, a suffocating accumulation of half-hearted policies and unhelpful administrative decisions hampered progress on listing, applied artificial limits not implied in the relevant statutes and, all too frequently, allowed the demolition of valuable buildings which had been correctly listed.

With all their faults (and they should not be understated), the remarkable thing about the initial lists was that they worked as well as they did. They were the work of dedicated scholars and they stood up to close examination (at public inquiries, for example) more often than they yielded to it. They also provided an effective springboard for the more sensitive building preservation policies that began to evolve from the mid-1960s onward.

The work was initiated by the Permanent Secretary, Anthony R Wagner (Sir Anthony Wagner, then Clarenceux, later Garter King of Arms), and directed within the new Ministry of Town and Country Planning by S R Garton, an ex-Ministry of Works architect. The selection criteria were formulated with the advice of the Minister's expert advisory group, known as the Maclagan Committee, and drawn up by one of their number, the leading architectural historian, John Summerson.

The qualities of the initial statutory lists can be traced directly back to a document which combined extensive knowledge, a clear philosophy and much common sense in one grey-covered, cyclostyled official paper: the *Instructions to Investigators for the Listing of Buildings of Special Architectural or Historic Interest under Section 42 of the Town and Country Planning Act 1944.*

Much of the original document is now of limited interest (you do not need to be taken through its account of the legislative background at that time, notes on the writing of list descriptions or instructions for collecting travelling expenses) but Chapters 2 and 3 contain excellent material, extracts from which are set out below. A great deal of what was said in 1946 is still relevant today and some parts contain ideas that were not to bear fruit until years later. The *Instructions* were an historical landmark. Their influence can still be detected in Planning Policy Guidance Note (PPG) 15 in 1994.

I have numbered the paragraphs for ease of reference. The emphases in particular passages of the original text are mine.

Instructions to Investigators: March 1946
CHAPTER 2

The administrative uses of the lists

2.1 It is certain that the section 42 lists, once in existence, will be used in many ways which cannot now be foreseen. Already possibilities are apparent which were not contemplated at the time when the sections were framed. For instance, occasion has arisen to compile lists of towns, villages, and areas, of special amenity from the architectural point of view. At present such lists can be based on no more than general impressions and recollections, but if the Section 42 lists were in existence, they could be looked through town by town and village by village and the proportion of listed buildings to the total worked out. In a rough and ready way at least this would give a statistical basis for what we are seeking and it might be possible to define a village of special amenity as one which had more than such and such a percentage of its buildings listed.

2.2 Because it cannot be foreseen to what uses lists may in the future be put it is the more important to take as wide a view as possible of their scope while they are in process of compilation, but the wider the view taken the more important it becomes to guard against the consequent risk that there may hereafter be uncertainty as to just what considerations have and have not been taken into account. In the next chapter an attempt will be made to set out the different types of special interest in buildings which it appears relevant to look for. This may not be exhaustive or may be too wide and suggestions for its amendment will be welcomed. Unless the contrary is stated in a specific instance it must be assumed that just these considerations and no others form the basis of the lists submitted. Because of the urgency of the risks of destruction which they are designed so far as possible to forestall, *the compilation of the lists must be carried out in haste* and therefore superficially. It will, for instance, seldom be possible to give time to inspect the interior of a building ...

2.1 and 2.2. Section 42 of the 1944 Act was the first to impose a duty on the relevant Minister (now the Secretary of State for National Heritage) to prepare lists of buildings of 'special architectural or historic interest'. Its terms have survived with little material amendment through all subsequent amending and consolidating legislation

The insistence in **2.2** that the lists needed to be compiled 'in haste' to avert threats of destruction was, as we have already remarked, thoroughly frustrated by later political and administrative failures, but in the pale dawn of 1946, the Instructions were blazing a remarkable trail.

It is clear from the paragraphs quoted above that the author of the Instructions anticipated that they could have uses beyond the protection of individual buildings. A number of speakers in the Parliamentary debates on the 1944 Bill had emphasised the importance of protecting complete environments as well as individual buildings. From the very first paragraph the author can be seen to be looking forward to the evaluation of whole areas for conservation in a way which foreshadows the Loi Malraux of 1962 and the Civic Amenities Act of 1967 (see note below on para **3.22**).

CHAPTER 3

The varieties of special interest

3.1 to 3.23 represent the view from 1946 of the ground I have attempted to cover in my Chapters 4 and 5.

> 3.1 The Act speaks of special architectural and historic interest and any building to be listed may have both, but must have one or the other kind of interest. Of course in a great measure they coexist. Most of the buildings which interest the architect also interest the historian and conversely, but the two kinds of interest combine in very different proportions and ways, between the extreme cases where one or the other only is in question. Under each head, the historical and the architectural, several distinct approaches or criteria can be recognised which it would certainly not be easy but is probably not necessary to reduce to common terms. So long as a building has special interest from any of the following points of view it can properly be listed or at least submitted for listing, since the lists put in by investigators will undergo a certain degree of censorship at Headquarters.

3.1 Note the writer's comments on the relationship between architectural and historic interest. In practice, the lists as approved by a succession of Ministers concentrated heavily on architectural interest and (at least so far as eighteenth century and later buildings are concerned) it has always been easier to defend buildings whose interest can be described principally in terms of their architectural and physical qualities.

3.2 *The first and clearest case is that of the building which is a work of art, the product of a distinct and outstanding creative mind.* There can be no doubt that every such building should be listed and that efforts should be made to preserve every one of them. This class includes not merely the greater national monuments but such minor masterpieces as Lindsey House, Lincoln's Inn Fields; the Jacobean Hunting Lodge at Sherborne, Gloucestershire; Abingdon Town Hall; the Church of St Mary Woolnoth; the Custom House, King's Lynn; 44 Berkeley Square; Wick House, Richmond, Surrey; or 1 Palace Green, Kensington.

3.2 The buildings named in the last sentence may appear to be an off-the-cuff selection, but they could hardly have been better chosen. It would have been all too easy at this point to produce a drumroll of 'greater national monuments' (the Royal palaces, Chatsworth, Blenheim, Strawberry Hill, St George's Hall…) with no more than a passing reference to the existence of 'minor masterpieces'. By singling out, for example, Lindsey House and 44 Berkeley Square, the point was made that the investigators were expected to approach their pioneering work in an inquiring and scholarly way, looking well beyond the obvious.

3.3 The next type is that of a building which is *not a distinct creation in this sense but possesses in a pronounced form the characteristic virtues of the school of design which produced it,* such as Eagle House, Mitcham; Cheyne Row, Chelsea; or the Paragon, Blackheath.

3.4 A third type of building which falls into neither of the above classes yet may qualify for listing on aesthetic grounds is the *outstanding composition of fragmentary beauties welded together by time and good fortune,* such a building as St James's Palace; Bisham Abbey; or the Deanery at Winchester.

3.2 and 3.3 together with the planned groups highlighted in **3.10** below, account for a large proportion of all listed buildings.

3.4 touches on a type of building whose qualities (notwithstanding the obvious importance of the examples he cites) can be quite difficult to define and defend. The Instructions sharpen our understanding by providing us with a splendidly simple definition. Faced with the scornful dismissal of an accretive building as 'a mishmash of alterations and additions of a variety of periods, unattributable as a whole to any architect of distinction, an architectural mess that should never have been listed', you may reply with confidence that, following the example of the listing investigators, you have analysed its special interest in meticulous detail and find it to be 'an outstanding composition of ... etc'.

> 3.5 Whether the interest of a building whose importance derives from its place in the history of architecture should be called architectural or historical or both is a matter of no importance but there probably are buildings which fall into this class and no other, *buildings whose sole but real value is that they exemplify a link in the chain of architectural development which if they were to perish would not be represented or represented so well.* Nicholas Barbon's houses in Bedford Row, Strawberry Hill, Dance's Guildhall front, or Thackeray's house in Palace Green, Kensington, might be examples.
>
> 3.6 In this class should be included those *architectural freaks* which have sufficient character to be of interest, such as the triangular lodge at Rushton, the Pagoda at Kew or the Tattingstone Wonder.
>
> 3.7 It must be understood that Architectural History for our purpose includes not only the history of architectural design but equally the history of structural, including engineering, technique, and that for our purpose a steel bridge is as much a building as a cathedral. *Certain industrial buildings* are landmarks (whether we call them architectural or historical makes no matter) of *the mechanical and industrial revolution*, and thus ought certainly to be listed, though it may be that the investigators will wish to seek specialist advice in the matter. Examples are the iron bridge at Ironbridge, the Colebrookedale [sic] Ironworks, Burton's Conservatory at Kew and the roofs of St Pancras Station and Lime Street Station, Liverpool.

3.7 The *Instructions* are again well ahead of their time in recognising the importance of industrial landmarks. Industrial archaeology was an uninvented term in 1946. The roof of St Pancras Station, which is singled out for mention, did not, in fact, enjoy statutory protection until another twenty years had passed.

> 3.8 At this point attention should be drawn to the absence from our terms of reference of any lower limit of date. *We may list buildings down to the present moment but we must of course be increasingly selective as the present day is approached.* It may be said very roughly that down to about 1725 buildings should be listed which survive in anything

> like original condition. Between that date and 1800 the greater number of buildings should probably be listed though selection will be necessary. Between 1800 and 1850 listing should be confined to buildings of definite quality and character. From 1850 down to 1914 only outstanding works should be included and since 1914 none unless the case seems very strong and it appears possible that the building may not be brought to light by central research. It is, however, desirable that *the selection of buildings for the last 150 years should comprise without fail the principal works of the principal architects* and to some extent it may be possible to secure this by central research. The results will, however, have in every case to be sent to the local investigator for checking on the spot.

3.8 A version of **3.8**, with minor modifications, was for many years incorporated into all explanations of listing policy. Paragraph 6.11 of PPG 15 (1994) was still remarkably similar.

The words 'selection' and 'selective' in **3.8** and **3.9** look innocent enough, but they should carry a warning light. The question of selection is, of course, raised as soon as any kind of inventorisation is attempted and it seems perfectly reasonable to insist that higher standards should be applied where the population being examined is a relatively large one. This was the thinking behind **3.8**, but if there is to be selection it must be seen to have been made on a wholly rational, qualitative basis. I remember a group of theatre historians being asked many years ago, to advise on the listing of theatre buildings. They assumed (and the error is a common one) that they were being asked which ones should be preserved. Looking at numbers of buildings with more or less equal claims for listing they decided ' to exercise restraint' and make a selection. Quite apart from the fact that the owner of a building arbitrarily singled out in this way could reasonably feel heartily aggrieved, such a selection might have had the effect of writing off perfectly preservable buildings before any decision on their future needed to be taken. Selection for listing is on quality alone, since what one is doing is identifying buildings with a claim for preservation.

The words 'anything like their original condition' were given too much emphasis during the compilation of the initial lists, leading to many buildings which would now be regarded as precious survivals being dismissed as 'altered' and relegated to the supplementary list (see commentary on **3.13** and **Grading** below). Similarly, the requirement that, post-1850, only 'outstanding works' should be listed resulted in the loss or fragmentation of complete later nineteenth-century developments of real architectural quality.

The further, apparently reasonable, admonition that 'the selection of buildings for the last 150 years should comprise without fail the principal works of the principal architects' has inevitably been moderated by the state of architectural scholarship at any given time. Sensitivities are sharpened by additions to the armoury of knowledge and the list of 'principal' architects is now rather longer than it would have been in 1946. A tendency to list approved names rather than evaluating the buildings themselves was accentuated when 20th century buildings came to be considered. Lutyens, for example, known to and admired by scholars, was regarded as listable while, at the same time, significant but less studied contemporaries of his were not.

The writer's statement that 'we may list buildings down to the present moment' (he mentions in **3.9** wartime pill boxes, then less than ten years old) got thoroughly overlaid with the muddy strata of subsequent administrative rulings during the following decades. Years of agonising over the problems of listing 'later' buildings led to what now look like panic moves to make good past neglect. The decision in 1970 to list 50 inter-war Modern Movement buildings might be seen in this light.

It is worth noting at this stage that, whatever listing practices, good or bad, may have evolved over the years, the Act applies only one test – the building must be of special architectural or historic interest. The comparatively recent (1987), not too rigidly applied, 'thirty year' rule is still arbitrary but has the merit of being a straight cut-off, easy to understand and not subject to the changing winds of fashion.

3.9   Coming now to pure *historic interest*, it is possible to distinguish two main aspects, which may be called the *evidential*, and the *sentimental*. The Gothic ruins of abbey or castle, a matter of sentiment only to the tourist, are valuable to the historian as first class evidence of the religious, social or military organisation of their period, and so with the dovecote, the windmill, the warehouse, the Martello Tower or the recent pill-box. It is obvious that as evidence for history practically all old buildings are of direct and substantial value, the slums as much as Mayfair, and further, that the substantial preservation of a whole village, say, is more helpful than that of the same number of houses spread over a county. On the other hand it is obviously essential to be selective.

3.9 But not so obvious, perhaps, how the selection should be made. Sentiment comes up again in 3.16

> 3.10 Under this heading the *sociological interest* of buildings, only now beginning to be seriously studied, has a very important place. There are, in every part of the country small buildings, particularly farmhouses, of regional style, reflecting the yeoman's activity and life in the sixteenth and seventeenth centuries; a wide range of characteristic examples of these should be preserved. In the more remote and thinly populated regions such as the Welsh and Northern Uplands, moreover, examples survive unaltered of cottages and farmhouse types which preserve the living and working arrangements characteristic of very remote periods, often indeed periods much more remote than those of the actual erection of the building in question since a Welsh seventeenth-century building may reflect arrangements prevalent in England far back in the Middle Ages. It is not possible that the present urgent listing should include the archaeological investigation necessary to map out the distribution and nature of these regional types on which alone a final assessment of the relative importance of their examples can be based. But the investigators ought at any rate to be aware of the existence of this problem and in so far as they can recognise a regional type, map its distribution and note its best examples and they will add conspicuously to the value of our material. It should be added that from this point of view unaltered original condition is a factor of special importance. It is, of course, well understood that this archaeological interest must often be at war with the interest of the adaptation of buildings for modern living. Indeed the neglected or decayed building which the Medical Officer of Health is most anxious to condemn will often be that which interests the archaeologists most. This conflict is not one which investigators will be called upon to attempt to solve. But if they will say what buildings are of interest and in what degree, they will have afforded part of the basis on which others must attempt to solve it.

3.10 The idea of protecting conditions reflecting the living arrangements characteristic of former times was, again, an advanced view, but the author suggested no more than that the investigators should be aware of the problem. He was well aware of the limits of the listing survey. There was little possibility of site-specific detailed research being undertaken and interiors could hardly ever be inspected (see **2.2** above).

The reference to possible conflicts between the interests of preservation and the powerful legal procedures designed to accelerate demolition assumed increasing significance in the post-war years. It was, of course, true that the listing investigators were not called upon to find solutions to such problems but, unhappily, neither was anyone else. The highly efficient steamroller of slum clearance flattened whole populations of buildings that would now be regarded as listable and excellent candidates for improvement.

> 3.11 Under the statute, as soon as possible after listing, the Minister has to serve a notice on every owner or occupier of a listed building. For this and other obvious reasons of administrative convenience the normal unit of listing will be the individual dwelling house or other property, *but it may often happen that the unit of architectural or historic interest is not the individual house but the whole context of which it forms a part*, e.g. a classical terrace of houses such as the Royal Crescent, Bath, is a single architectural unit and should be listed and graded as such. This point is of especial importance for many planned streets and terraces of the first half of the nineteenth century in which it might be difficult to say that any single house was of special architectural interest though it is quite certain that the street as a whole does and will, so long as it can be preserved as a whole, possess such interest. This planned architectural group is the first type of group that has to be borne in mind.

3.11 The argument set out here is clearly valid for all periods, not only the first half of the nineteenth century, but contemporary opinion was not ready for a broader view. See commentary on **3.8** regarding the effect of listing practice on later planned estates.

> 3.12 The next step is what may be called *the accidental or pictorial architectural group* where, by the good fortune of architectural good manners or a prevalent unity of feeling and approach at the time and place of building, a row of separately planned and built houses blend together into a group which in its wholeness gives a greater value to many of its members than they would have if they stood alone. Such groups of seventeenth, eighteenth and early nineteenth-century buildings will often be seen in the High Streets of ancient market towns. In such a context it will often be desirable for the sake of its value to the group to list a building which might not be listed if it

stood by itself. There is a nice distinction to be observed here; a building must not be listed merely because its neighbours are good and one is afraid that if it were to be demolished it would be replaced by some vulgar monstrosity which would not be tolerable, and least of all in good company. The design of new buildings can and should be controlled under general planning powers and it is not therefore proper to place on the statutory list a building under Section 42 simply to ensure a congruity of neighbourhood which could as well be achieved in a new building. It must be possible to say that the old building, however plain and ordinary in its kind, has some quality in relation to the context which no new building could have.

3.13 There will probably be difficult borderline cases where investigators' feeling is that what is worth preserving somehow *is a general character, in a street, town or quarter of a town, which is the cumulative effect of the grouping or repetition of a type of building*, of which it is hard to say that any single specimen is more important than any other and yet it is certain that some, if not too many, could without real loss be spared. It is the Ministry's view that, while such buildings as these ought to receive special consideration and protection, this should be given rather by simple notice from the Ministry to the Local Authority and by the normal exercise of planning control than by Statutory listing under Section 42 of the Act. Investigators are therefore asked to exclude from their draft Statutory Lists but to note on *Supplementary Lists* buildings which have in their view cumulative group or character value, but which have not that degree of intrinsic architectural or historic interest which would naturally be called special interest. Group interest is not excluded from the Statutory Lists but the test set out above must be applied to it.

3.14 The *group* whether for statutory or supplementary list purposes need not necessarily be a street group. A group of cottages round a green or in the open country comes as properly under this heading; and under it may be brought also the building whose value lies in the part it plays in a landscape. The more usual and obvious case of this kind is that of the folly obelisk, ruin and the like deliberately designed to play a part in the landscape composition. Where the avenue or vista that building was designed to terminate still exists, the building retains a value in that relation, regardless of any other consideration whatever, and may for that reason alone deserve listing.

3.12 to 3.14 Group value was recognised in the lists from the beginning, but many second rank 'group' buildings were relegated to the 'supplementary list'. The writer here seems to point forward, once again, to the conservation area idea. His suggestion that the design of replacements for buildings of group value could safely be left to planning control was, however, highly optimistic. The very idea can still trigger off angry argument between those who believe that all forms of aesthetic control are anathema and those who think that a coherent group, notwithstanding the variable quality of its parts, should be protected as if it were one listed building. More than half a century later this argument has yet to be won and lost (see Chapter 10 on Contexts).

The now extinct supplementary list referred to in **3.13** – which acknowledged that a building had some qualities worthy of recognition, but gave it no statutory protection whatever – was a grave mistake (see notes on **Grading**, below).

3.15 A rarer case is that of *the building which, by happy chance, contributes to the natural landscape*. It is not positively asserted that there are cases of this kind in which listing is proper, but they are certainly not ruled out a priori, and if an investigator feels that he can make a case for listing on this ground he should do so.

3.16 The *sentimental* interest is more elusive and yet *sentiment is probably the strongest single thread in our interest in the past*. This may be entirely specific, arising from a particular event or a particular person, e.g. the scene of the Rye House plot or Keats's house at Hampstead; or less specific as connected with a class of well-known persons or a succession of events, e.g. the Albert Hall, or the Stock Exchange; or merely general, e.g. the feeling excited by prehistoric remains, Roman roads, or mediaeval abbeys. This historic sentiment is at once a very complex and comprehensive feeling. At its lowest it is an aspect of national self-respect, weak in early societies which rapidly destroy their past, but growing ever stronger with the lengthening of time, and most particularly in a society like ours whose historical development has not been catastrophic. The older it grows the more it looks back to its youth. But, of course, it can be a great deal more than this, old buildings having the power to kindle the historical imagination in a way denied to documents which supplement them.

3.16 Note that sentiment is here discussed at length and not dismissed as a minor issue. Building conservation today, in all its aspects, from historical research, through physical investigation techniques to the scientific study of building pathology, is massively more sophisticated than it was half a century ago. The first sentence of this paragraph, nevertheless, contains an unchanging truth. Sentiment is probably the strongest single thread in our interest in the past.

3.17 Where such interest consists in a personal association, the first question which must be asked is how well or really that association is authenticated. Local tradition is not always a trustworthy guide and where investigators, having examined the evidence available to them, still remain doubtful, they should put down what they know and refer the matter to Headquarters. There are cases, however, where *the continuing belief in a tradition may itself have constituted an historic interest*, even though the original tradition may be baseless. This is not the place to enter upon discussion of the authenticity of Shakespeare's birthplace at Stratford-on-Avon but it can unhesitatingly be said that even were it proved absolutely that Shakespeare had never entered the house, nevertheless the existence since Garrick's time of an intensive cult centering upon that house would constitute an historic interest amply sufficient to place the house in the first class of the lists.

3.18 A similar argument may perhaps in certain cases, justify the listing of buildings whose association is with characters or events in fiction, such as the birthplace of John Halifax, Gentleman, at Tewkesbury or the White Horse Inn at Ipswich where Mr Pickwick's room is shown.

3.19 Again it should be asked how important in national or local history was the person in question and how close was his association with the building? In particular, how far is it likely that he was conscious of the building as a factor in his life? The Brontes' life in Haworth Parsonage is evidently of first importance as a dominating element in their experience reflected throughout their work. Less dominating and intense, but not unlike in kind, are the associations of Blake with Felpham, Ruskin with Denmark Hill, Darwin with Downe, Dickens with Gadshill or Tennyson with Farringford. But it is difficult to feel that the same interest attaches to the transient and little remembered associations of lodgers or tenants upon short lease, however distinguished, with town houses in London or Bath. This kind of association is not to be ignored but they should be looked at more critically.

3.20 *A special kind of interest perhaps attaches where the historical personage either built or substantially altered or extended the house in question.* In such a case it may bear upon it physical marks of his mind and taste which are interesting. Thomas Hardy's house, Max Gate, is a case in point; Sir John Soane's house would be another were it not obvious that there is there a very positive and overriding architectural interest. *Associations with historical events and phases of historical development* may afford good grounds for listing, such as those of the Ship Hotel at Greenwich where the whitebait dinners were held, the manager's house at Vauxhall Gardens, now St Peter's Vicarage, or the booking office of the Stockton and Darlington Railway at Stockton.

3.20 Sadly, one of the prime examples of associational interest cited here, the Ship Hotel, was never included in any list, was war damaged and subsequently demolished.

3.21 An instance which may fall between this category and that of sociological interest is that of the houses on the Charterville allotments near Witney, the fragmentary relic of a projected Chartist Utopia.

3.22 Finally it is necessary to draw attention to the special value of whole groups from the historical point of view. The preservation of the character of a whole town such as Conway or of the eighteenth-century character of Bath has a historical value almost of a different order from that attaching to the preservation of individual houses within these groups. From other points of view a single eighteenth-century building of moderate quality acquires extra value from being placed in an otherwise uninteresting wilderness of bleak modernity, but from this particular historical point of view the case is reversed and the maxim is 'to him that hath shall be added'.

3.23 An attempt like this to express in words what cannot be so expressed must necessarily dwell disproportionately on abnormal and borderline cases for these, after all, are where difficulties occur; once the limits of our special interest are understood, what falls within them may be taken more or less for granted. But it should probably be said that the special cases discussed in detail in this chapter will provide only a fraction of the total number of listed buildings. The great bulk and staple of the work will deal with clear and undoubted examples of fine buildings and it may be guessed that numerically the eighteenth century will (in total, though not in all localities) have a clear preponderance over any other.

Grading

Chapter 4 and Appendix IV of the *Instructions* deal with grading. It may, perhaps, be instructive to look at a few brief extracts, to see how the grading system was first conceived:

> In order that the Ministry may have some guidance on the relative importance of different buildings and the degree of effort which ought in each case to be made to secure preservation in the face of any threat, every building should be graded I, II or III. The *Statutory Lists* will comprise the buildings in Grades I and II, the *Supplementary Lists* those in Grade III. In Grade I should be placed buildings of such importance that their demolition should *in no case* be allowed; in Grade II buildings whose preservation is a matter of national interest so that though it may be that now and then the preservation of a Grade II building will have to give way before some other yet more important consideration … yet the Ministry will, in each case, take such steps as are in its power to avoid the necessity of this and where no conflict of *national* interest can be shown will take such positive steps as are open to it to secure the building's preservation.

Note that matters of less than national concern were not seen as a reasons for allowing demolition of a Grade II building.

> In Grade III will be placed (1) buildings of architectural or historic interest which do not, however, rise to the degree properly qualified as special, (2) buildings which so contribute to a general effect that the planning authority ought in the preparation and administration of its plan to regard this effect as an asset worth trying to keep …
>
> The investigator will find that in areas which are architecturally poor he will tend to lower his standards and, for instance, place in Grade II buildings which in another area he would consign to Grade III. This tendency is reasonable and should not be over-corrected. The strictly local value of a building can properly be given weight…
>
> There will be a fringe of buildings below the standard of Grade III, for the preservation of which there may nevertheless at some time be pressure … Where the investigator is doubtful whether a particular building should be listed or not, it will be helpful if in the draft list he will note it but grade it IV.

Grading in four categories was probably a necessary tool in compiling the initial lists and a grading apparatus, although significantly improved since 1946, has survived to the present time. That this is another area where widening knowledge can lead to sharpening sensibility is illustrated by the regular upgradings that now occur, most often from Grade II to Grade II* (the latter being a somewhat later refinement to the system).

The important thing about the lists today is that, regardless of grade, the statutory provisions apply to all and in the same degree to all. The creation of a non-statutory supplementary list was, as we have already noted, a serious error and even this feeble list contained only those buildings the investigators had allocated to Grade III (astonishingly, Victorian prodigy buildings like St Pancras Station and the Midland Hotel were originally consigned to this dangerous limbo). If Grade III was bad news, Grade IV was worse. It fell out of sight completely. Many of the buildings noted as Grade IV now exist only as evocative photographs in local and national archives.

It was not possible in 1946 to foresee what enormous development pressures would come to bear in the following decades. Relatively few planning authorities made effective use of their powers under the 1944–7 Planning Acts to make building preservation orders in respect of statutory, let alone supplementary, listed buildings. In many areas, all of the supplementary list buildings had been demolished by the mid-1960s and the losses nearly everywhere were massive. Non-statutory lists and 'local' lists are useless in the hands of incompetent or unwilling controllers. In the 1950s and 1960s the words 'only on the supplementary list' were used as much by planning authorities as by developers to justify demolition.

In conclusion

There are, of course, lessons to be learned from the unperceived weaknesses in the Instructions. The mistake of inventorising buildings which the Minister believed 'should receive special consideration and protection', while failing to give them statutory protection, has been noted, but the more fundamental error was perhaps that of giving too much weight to 'original' condition (**3.8**). The enjoyable scholarly sport of awarding medals to some buildings and withholding them from others of not much less interest actually diverted the purpose of the legislation, producing a time bomb which eventually devastated many architecturally unified areas. The supplementary list cemetery is packed full of buildings which would

now be highly regarded but which had to be dismissed by the listing inves
tigators as 'altered'.

Despite all such reservations, the student is advised to study the quoted
portions of this text in detail. It is now an historical document in its own
right, but the thinking behind it is of immediate relevance. It is easy, with
the benefit of hindsight, to criticise it for what are now seen to be its flaws,
but it remains a remarkable statement which, for breadth of vision and
clarity of thought, is hard to fault. Like the SPAB *Manifesto*, its influence
has reached across the years.

Further Reading

Angus Acworth and Sir Anthony Wagner, wrote an article on '25 Years of
Listing' in the *Architectural Review*, November 1970. Although edited into
third person form, this has the immediacy of a first hand account by two
of the principal players of the 1940s. An account (by John Harvey, Martin
Robertson and others) of the evolution of listing policy and practice from
1947 to 1993, appeared in *Ancient Monuments Society Transactions* Vol. 37
(1993). This describes some earlier attempts at inventorisation and tables
of statistics corrected to 1988. Professor Andrew Saint's chapter 'How
Listing Happened' in Michael Hunter (ed.) *Preserving the Past*, 1996, is the
most important recent study, containing many insights into the history
and progress of listing.

Education for Conservation

In 1993 the General Assembly of ICOMOS adopted *Guidelines for Education and Training in the Conservation of Monuments, Ensembles and Sites*. The guidelines recognise that 'many different professions need to collaborate within the common discipline of conservation ... and require proper education and training in order to guarantee good communication and coordinated action.'

It is a short document and paragraph 5 contains perhaps the clearest statement yet made of the varied skills needed for successful conservation. It says that education and training should produce from a range of professionals, conservationists who are able to:

a. read a monument, ensemble or site and identify its emotional, cultural and use significance;
b. understand the history and technology of monuments, ensembles or sites in order to define their identity, plan for their conservation, and interpret the results of this research;
c. understand the setting of a monument, ensemble or site, their contents and surroundings, in relation to other buildings, gardens or landscapes;
d. find and absorb all available sources of information relevant to the monument, ensemble or site being studied;
e. understand and analyse the behaviour of monuments, ensembles and sites as complex systems;
f. diagnose intrinsic and extrinsic causes of decay as a basis for appropriate action;
g. inspect and make reports intelligible to non-specialist readers of monuments, ensembles or sites, illustrated by graphic means such as sketches and photographs;

h. know, understand and apply UNESCO conventions and recommenda-
    tions, and ICOMOS and other recognized Charters, regulations and
    guidelines;
i. make balanced judgements based on shared ethical principles, and
    accept responsibility for the long-term welfare of cultural heritage;
j. recognize when advice must be sought and define the areas of need of
    study by different specialists, e.g. wall paintings, sculpture and objects
    of artistic and historical value, and/or studies of materials and systems;
k. give expert advice on maintenance strategies, management policies and
    the policy framework for environmental protection and preservation
    of monuments and their contents, and sites;
l. document works executed and make same accessible;
m. work in multi-disciplinary groups using sound methods;
n. be able to work with inhabitants, administrators and planners to
    resolve conflicts and to develop conservation strategies appropriate to
    local needs, abilities and resources.

The *Guidelines* come down heavily in favour of multi-disciplinary courses
and this must, clearly, be the way ahead. There are no conservators, pure
and simple. There are architect conservators, surveyor conservators, engi-
neer conservators, planner conservators, artist conservators, scientist conservators, and so on, through all the professions involved. They must be
able to work together, focusing their individual skills on to a single objective and it is therefore highly desirable that their education should, from
the beginning, be closely coordinated. The design of multi-disciplinary
courses is, however, not a simple matter and it is not helped by the fact that
most of the professional institutions regard conservation as a fringe spe-
cialisation to be acquired solely by post-graduate study, if it is acquired at
all. Despite the fact that most members of (in particular) the building professions will find themselves dealing with old buildings some of the time
and some of them all of the time, first degree courses very rarely acknowl-
edge the significance of this work.

It follows that the intake on any conservation course is likely to be
varied not only as to original discipline but also in the kinds of experience
and acquired skills the students bring with them. Even within a single discipline there is unlikely to be a common starting line, while in all disciplines there may be a need to overcome some aspects of past professional
conditioning. Architects, for example, traditionally the leaders of the team,
must be prepared to subdue their carefully nurtured creative instincts in
order to enter the minds of the creators of the buildings they are dealing

with. Engineers must accept that some problems are made less amenable to solution by being reduced to what can be calculated. Surveyors must become as absorbed by the history of architecture and construction as by the economics and technology of repair.

What all good conservators, across all professions, must have in common is a comprehensive curiosity about the nature of buildings and places, a concern for factual precision in describing and recording them, an analytical approach to problems which leaves no relevant fact out of consideration and a determination to find solutions that satisfy conservation imperatives. There is now a wide choice of post-graduate courses that nurture these qualities and look for a varied intake, but however good their formal programmes may be, students will need throughout their working lives to attend to their own continuing education.

The Canadian *Code of Ethics* (Appendix 5) exhorts the conservation professional to recognise his or her limitations and the special skills and knowledge of others, but this should not be taken as encouragement to pass over a problem completely to other specialists as soon as their skills are called for. Cooperation between the various disciplines is not only the key to successful conservation, it is also of immense instructional value for all concerned. Every encounter, whether in a formal meeting or at a coffee machine, can take on the character of a symposium, ranging over the general as well as the particular. It is in this kind of inquiring environment that philosophies appropriate to the tasks in hand are most likely to evolve.

'A Permanent Agency'

In 1905 Baldwin Brown set the pieces on the board for a game that, so far as Britain was concerned, had hardly begun to be played. No legislation for the defence of monuments could come into effect, he said unless there was 'a certain force of intelligent belief' among the people that there was a need for it. 'What is required' he said 'Is some permanent agency representing the public mind at its best and always kept in working order.'

No such agency existed at that time and Brown was clearly not optimistic about the chances of official action to remedy the situation. 'If we judged from the charges to the account of monuments in our annual budgets' he said, 'We should say that in Britain government did less for monuments than is done in any other European country.' The ancient Monuments Acts, he declared, had become almost a dead letter. No Inspector of Ancient Monuments had been appointed to succeed General Pitt Rivers, who had died in 1900. Britain was almost alone in Europe in having taken no action to prepare a national register of monuments and, in so far as any inventorisation had been attempted, it had been the work of private agencies and a few municipal bodies, notably the London County Council (LCC).

The LCC, created in 1889, was the first democratically elected body with extensive powers over the entire metropolis. In the first decade of its existence, the LCC hosted a conference on listing, obtained special powers to acquire and preserve historic buildings, resolved to examine the possibility of action in the case of threatened destruction and voted money for the publication of detailed records of buildings in association with the voluntary Committee for the Survey of the Memorials of Greater London. In 1901, it took over the work of the Royal Society of Arts in fixing plaques to houses with important historical associations.

All these activities led to the slow evolution of a cadre of skilled professionals. The first acquisitions of historic buildings from the 1890s onward (often they were buildings associated with the preservation of vulnerable open spaces) was followed in 1900 by the council's first major restoration work, a seventeenth-century tavern at the Inner Temple gateway in Fleet Street. By 1986, when the LCC's successor body, the Greater London Council, was abolished, the council had nearly 1,000 historic buildings under its direct care, had made measured records of some thousands of buildings, was the sole publisher of the learned *Survey of London* volumes, and had unique powers of control over all the listed buildings in London. Its Historic Buildings Division had seventy architects, surveyors, historians and supporting staff. Nearly all the varied skills needed to deal with every aspect of research, physical care and control were available, working closely together in one unit in one location.

On a national scale, although official activity accelerated after World War II (at first notably in listing) and rather more significantly after the mid-1960s, progress was still patchy. Despite the manifest popularity of preservation in the broadest sense, failures of political will continued to delay progress. The need for some kind of consolidation of powers and responsibilities for all the varied aspects of care and protection became painfully clear over time but no attempt was made to create a new structure until 1983. In that year the Historic Buildings and Monuments Commission for England (English Heritage) was created. Similar reforms were to take place in Scotland and Wales with the creation of Historic Scotland and CADW.

These were vitally important moves. English Heritage and its Scottish and Welsh equivalents brought together into single, unified bodies, nearly all official conservation activities, nationwide.

English Heritage, the largest of the new national organisations, advised by a body of distinguished commissioners and staffed by expert architects, historians, surveyors, engineers, archaeologists and scientists, is reliant on government grant-in-aid, but is otherwise free to set its own priorities and fight its own corner. It is a powerful body, the first point of contact for all special interest groups and also the principal source of advice for the use of those powers which necessarily and legally have to remain with a Secretary of State.

From the outset, English Heritage has had groups and divisions dealing with properties in care, listing surveys, listed building consent casework, ancient monuments scheduling and consents, redundant churches, buildings at risk, recording and rescue archaeology. It took over the National

Monuments Record, set up a laboratory, carried out scientific investigations, made repair grants and started work on a register of historic gardens.

The way in which the organisation developed and operated in the years following is a matter of record. In 1999 it commenced a merger with the Royal Commission on Historic Monuments (England) (RCHME) and by 2002 it was recommended that it should take over responsibility for maritime heritage in English territorial waters. One of its important, easily overlooked, functions is in publication. Its conservation bulletins, research transactions and specialist studies are of particular benefit to practitioners and its burgeoning booklist covers a wide range of topics accessible to the general reader, ranging from a scholarly architectural history of *English Prisons*, through *Life in a Mediaeval Abbey* to the popular *Heritage Hikes*.

It can be said that we now have 'a permanent agency' of international stature, 'representing the public mind at its best'. Baldwin Brown could not for a moment have anticipated anything so advanced and effective. But weaknesses still remain in the apparatus of care and protection.

The idea that having set the highest standards at the highest levels, the rest can be delegated to local level is seductive (and very British) but it is not a recipe for guaranteed success. The public nearly everywhere shows great and growing concern for the better conservation of the environment, but local government has an extremely uneven record of performance. The most effective authorities take their responsibilities seriously and have excellent conservation teams, achieving outstanding results. At the other extreme are authorities that, regardless of local pressure, treat their role in listed building control as a tiresome burden, to be given a minimum of attention. Where such authorities employ specialised staff, they are fully aware that there is no compulsory requirement to act and feel that enough has been done if they simply attach a label to a sole, relatively junior officer in their planning department. In these circumstances, the conservation officer may strive to do a good job, but will frequently find his or her advice disregarded or overruled.

It is not enough to settle the big issues and oversee the most important buildings at national level and assume that 'less important matters of detail' can be left to bodies who may or may not be competent to deal with them. And the worst performers commonly have the greatest faith in their own competence.

Successful conservation, at individual case level, is about knowledge and attention to detail. Until planning authorities are required to maintain proper conservation units commensurate with their responsibilities (which may, paradoxically, be great where the heritage is most depleted) there will continue to be dismal and unnecessary failures. The creation of a national agency like English Heritage would have seemed ludicrously unlikely in the 1960s. We now need to plan the next equally unlikely reform.

Bibliography

The student is recommended to read all philosophical writings, including this study, with an extremely critical eye.

The need to proceed from a detailed understanding of each individual problem via logical argument to a philosophically defensible solution has been the constant *leitmotiv* of this book and the bibliography is designed to suit this end. Although relevant material can be found in other books than those listed here (and certainly in such specialised periodicals as the *Journal of Architectural Conservation*, Donhead) very few writers have dealt specifically and at length with philosophy. What follows, therefore, is a highly selective guide to a small number of studies which, in their different ways, should be found particularly useful and thought provoking. The reader looking for a wider-ranging bibliography of the whole field of building conservation is advised to refer to Professor Feilden's (1994) or Watt and Swallow's (1996) comprehensive listings.

This list is arranged chronologically.

Books

Professor G Baldwin Brown, *The Care of Ancient Monuments*, Cambridge University Press, Cambridge, 1905.

A key text of its time, concerned mainly with the development of formal protective measures rather than (as the short title might suggest) the physical care of monuments.

A R Powys, *Repair of Ancient Buildings*, SPAB, 1929 (reprinted 1981).

SPAB philosophy in practice. The Society had previously published *Guidelines* in 1903. Although some of the methods described now carry added notes in the light of later knowledge, the main text remains a valuable statement of the practical implications of the attitudes embodied in the Society's *Manifesto*.

Walter H Godfrey, *Our Building Inheritance,* Faber & Faber, London, 1944.

A polemical rather than philosophical work. It is now more of an historical document in its own right than a learning text. It was written near the end of the World War II, well before the statutory controls over historic buildings (as distinct from ancient monuments) were in place in Britain, but just as the first serious thought was being given to the conservation of historic towns as well as individual buildings. Godfrey was concerned with the importance of continuity in building technique and architectural tradition. He also argued that it made good sense to conserve the resource represented by old buildings at a time of straitened national circumstances. The historical context, however, frequently fades into the background, as he seems to address the conditions and problems of our own time.

Ian Nairn, *Outrage!,* Architectural Press, Oxford, 1955.

Probably the first and certainly the most effective post-war polemic on the mindless disfigurement of town and countryside. Its main concern was with architectural and environmental issues, but it promoted an awareness of visual qualities, which worked to the benefit of historic buildings and places. The shock produced by its original appearance in *Architectural Review* led to a Government minister calling a meeting with the author and publishers. The same author's *Counter Attack*, proposing remedies, appeared the following year, but many of the 'outrages' highlighted by Nairn in 1955 can still be observed today.

Jane Jacobs, *The Death and Life of Great American Cities,* Harmondsworth, New York, 1961.

A disturbing critique of the destructive and socially disruptive effects of much mid-twentieth century town planning. Jacobs looked at cities in a holistic way, pointing *inter alia* to 'the need for aged buildings', not at the time widely acknowledged in North America.

Racihel Carson, *Silent Spring,* Houghton Mifflin, Boston, Mass., 1962.

Carson, a biologist, was concerned with the natural rather than the built environment, underlining the intimate interaction between all forms of life on earth and the perilous results of ignoring the consequences of our interferences. Her chilling dissection of the 'modern, chemical drenched world' sounded an urgently needed alarm call. The warnings of both Carson and Jacobs (1961 above) have been powerful influences on conservators in all fields and are as relevant in the early twenty-first century as they were in the 1960s.

Roy Worskett, *The Character of Towns: An Approach to Conservation,* Oxford University Press, Oxford 1969.

One of the first modern works on area conservation.

Donald Insall, *Care of Old Buildings Today*, Architectural Press, Oxford, 1972.

One of a remarkably small number of such manuals, post-Powys (see above 1929), embodying the philosophy of a modern practitioner.

Jane Fawcett (ed.), *The Future of the Past*, 1976.

A series of essays, recommended mainly for those by Sir Nikolaus Pevsner, Osbert Lancaster and Jane Fawcett.

M W Thompson, *Ruins, Their Preservation and Display*, Colonnade British Museum (Publication), London, 1981.

A compact review, accessible to the non-archaeologist, dealing with attitudes to, as well as the treatment of ruins.

James Marston Fitch, *Historic Preservation: Curatorial Management of the Built World*, University Press Virginia, NY, 1982.

A wide-ranging and illuminating treatise by the founder of the first historic preservation programme in a North American university (Columbia NY). Many of the individual chapters are outstanding essays on the subjects they address (try, for example, Fitch on 'Cosmetic Consequences of Intervention'). Students with a serious interest in ideas and arguments can be recommended to put this book near the top of their reading list. The only disappointing feature is the index.

Sir Bernard Feilden, *Conservation of Historic Buildings*, Butterworth, Oxford, 1982, (revised and reprinted 1994).

The most authoritative and accessible standard work for conservation practitioners but noted here particularly because Chapter 1 'Introduction to architectural conservation' is greatly concerned with the philosophy and ethics of conservation. A comprehensive bibliography is provided.

Jukka Jokilehto, *History of Architectural Conservation*, Butterworth-Heinemann, Oxford, 1999.

Based on his 1986 PhD thesis, this is the definitive historical account, unlikely ever to be superseded. Jokilehto embraces all important movements and their leaders from Antiquity to the present day.

Christopher Brereton, *Repair of Historic Buildings: Advice on Principles and Methods*, English Heritage, London, 1991.

A short, sound introduction for the unspecialised reader.

Susan Macdonald (ed.), *Modern Matters: Principles and Practice in Conserving Recent Architecture*, Donhead, Shaftesbury, 1995.

The proceedings of an English Heritage conference with a series of papers by experts on various aspects of the protection and care of twentieth-century buildings. The contributions embrace philosophical, as well as practical issues, including such questions as the reconciliation of authenticity and repair in the conservation of modern architecture.

Michael Hunter (ed.), *Preserving the Past: the Rise of Heritage in Modern Britain*, Alan Sutton, 1996.

A history presented in the form of a series of essays by a team of experts. Every contribution illuminates the ways in which ideas about various aspects of conservation have developed.

David Watt and Peter Swallow, *Surveying Historic Buildings*, Donhead, Shaftesbury, 1996.

Essentially a practical manual, not much concerned with theoretical questions, but containing a particularly useful bibliography.

English Heritage, *Sustaining the Historic Environment: new perspectives on the future*, 1997.

Only 11 pages and described as 'a preliminary statement of policy', but amongst the best and most readable introductions to the subject.

David Lowenthal, *The Heritage Crusade and the Spoils of History*, Cambridge University Press, Cambridge, 1998.

Lowenthal is an academic who has examined the history and social and psychological significance of heritage movements (a previous study was *The Past is a Foreign Country*, 1985).

Martin Pawley, *Terminal Architecture*, 1998.

Pawley is a leading anti-conservationist. Chapter 5 of this book contains a devastating critique of the harmful effects, as he sees them, of conservationists and art historians on modern architecture.

Susan Macdonald (ed.), *Preserving Post-war Heritage*, Donhead, Shaftesbury, 1998.

> The proceedings of an English Heritage conference, with a series of papers looking at the special conservation problems and philosophical issues raised by comparatively recent buildings. Part of chapter 1 (by Alan Powers) counters Pawley's arguments (see above).

John Delafons, *Politics and Preservation: a policy history of the built heritage 1882–1996*, E. & F. Spon, London, 1999.

> The fullest historical account of British legislation and policies so far attempted.

Charters and Codes

The SPAB *Manifesto*, the *Venice Charter*, the *Burra Charter* and the Canadian *Code of Ethics* are extensively quoted and commented upon in Appendices 2, 3, 4 and 5. A number of other charters and codes are listed at the appropriate dates in the Chronology (Appendix 1). The full texts of many of them can be seen on the ICOMOS website: www.international.icomos.org

Last Words ...

To conclude this low Account of this magnificent Fabrick, but which indeed no words can illustrate as it ought to be, we shall only say, that it is a Building of that Magnitude and Extent, that even in those Ages which affected the erecting of Religious Structures, it took near two Centuries to complete; since which it has stood above three more, and hitherto escaped the Teeth of corroding Time by Wind and Weather; or , what is more destructive than either of them, Party Zeal. Let it be the Prayer of all good Men, that this glorious Building, the great Monument of our Forefathers' Piety, may never want a Governor less devoted to its Preservation than the last two actually were, and the present one hitherto has been: that this Fabrick may stand firm and transmit to late Posterity the Virtue of its Founders, and continue what has been, not only a singular Ornament to the City and these Northern Parts, but to the whole Kingdom.
Anon; from *An Accurate Description and History of the Cathedral and Metropolitan Church of St Peter York, from its first Foundation to the present Year*, Second edition 1783

And if some should say: 'These things must be; change must come and with it loss and disappointment; have faith in the future which will bring greater triumphs than in the past', I would answer that all this may be, but it is poor advice to cut away the lower part of the ladder before we have reached the top.
Walter H Godfrey, *Our Building Inheritance*, 1944

Of the 30,000 thatched cottages in Northern Ireland in 1950, just 120 are left.
Noted in *Context* (IHBC journal) March 2002

The older I get, the less I like about old buildings.
Lord Rogers 2002

Index

Page numbers in *italics* refer to illustrations.